CONTEMPLATION

words and silence for the Way Home

Stephen G Wright

For
My sister Jacqueline and my brother Alan

Contemplation – words and silence for the Way Home, first edition 2010 by Sacred Space Publications, Fell End, Mungrisdale, Cumbria, England CA11 0XR
Second edition 2017

British Library Cataloguing in Publication Data: A catalogue record for this book is available from the British Library.
ISBN 978-0-9560303-8-2

Design layout and typesetting by:-
Barry Marshall, BeCreative
Home Farm Office, Eamont Bridge, Penrith, Cumbria CA10 2BX
www.becreativecumbria.co.uk

If you listen carefully,
if you listen very carefully,
you can hear the universe
breathing
in
and out
at the same time.

Acknowledgements

My gratitude goes to Jean Gray, Jeannie Sayre-Adams, Dr Kenneth Sayre, Kristopher Drummond, Rev'd Tom Keighley and Rev'd Peter Dewey for reviewing and correcting the text. Ian Webster I thank for all the patient backroom work that enabled me to be lost in the computer without interruption. Barry Marshall's work through all the stages of production is deeply appreciated

Contents

A Letter from Home

Dear Unknown Friend,

When I last wrote to you, the letter turned out a little longer than I had planned. It became a book, *Coming Home*, passing on some of the rich teachings with which I had been blessed down the years. I mapped out some of the joys and pitfalls on the way Home, particularly the value of having four Soul Care approaches. Soul Foods (such as music, the arts, nature or scripture), Soul Communities (groups to support us and aid in discernment), Soul Friends (our spiritual directors and mentors) and Soul Works (meditation, prayer and going on retreat for example) provided the main themes and structure for that book. Readers of that first text may recall that I promised to let you have more information on one particular topic, a Soul Work, called contemplation.

So, here you have the companion volume to *Coming Home*. Sitting alongside *Yours, Faithfully* and *Beloved* and *Song and Dance for the Way Home*, it is a practical guide and at the same time a gathering of views on the subject from almost 2000 years of teaching.

I hope the words in this book will inspire, challenge and encourage you. You might keep notes in a reflective journal about your experiences and share them as grist to the mill with your Soul Friend and Soul Community. Remember that our inner work, and our testing and discernment of that work with others, is a valuable way of refining and deepening our spiritual life so that we enter into the full "fruits of the spirit" – of being more loving, more present, more connected and of more service to the world and the Divine. The discipline of practice and the willingness, in humility, to be open to the guidance of others make it less likely that we will become side-tracked, ego-inflated, self-regarding or caught up in the myriad pitfalls of spiritual awakening.

I have drawn primarily on the lives and works of Christian mystics and contemplatives both ancient and modern, for that is the tradition that has been passed to me. You may recall that I laid great emphasis in *Coming Home* on the value of drawing upon a tradition, although of course I did not instruct you as to which one. I just shared my experiences. I hope that, regardless of your religious and spiritual path, you will find guidance in the words of wisdom of the mystic-contemplatives I cite, for they illuminate in their own way the spiritual truths of contemplation found in all faiths. There may be different emphases and nuances, but the common ground outweighs these and is one of the powerful unifying forces drawing together traditions, which might otherwise be hostile to one another.

These early Christian contemplatives and mystics (and we will explore the differences and commonalities later) experienced God being revealed to them personally as well as being guided by scripture, the teachings of the church, scholarly study and the influences of the culture and traditions from which they emerged. Our times bring their own influences to bear upon this eternal unfolding of the Divine in the world and the mystic experience.

As we shall see, this emergence is not conducted in isolation atop some lonely mountain (although for some that may be at least a part of our Way), but with the essential principles in place that I explored in *Coming Home* – the need for Soul Friends, Soul Communities, Soul Works and Soul Foods. Indeed, as we shall see, the modern spiritual trend of individual exploration without boundaries is not recommended in this or any other of the companion books. Spiritual awakening is full of the joy of expanding consciousness, but it brings with it many struggles too, struggles that are not wisely kept to the solitary exploit. Our rewards and difficulties are best held in community and companionship. The contemplative, for example, follows a particular path classically described as purgative, illuminative and, finally, unitive. That is, a clearing out of our limited ego perceptions and agendas of life as we have lived it, an awakening to new vistas and potential of what life really is and a drawing closer into union with the Divine from which we are born into living life anew.

There is a wonderful paradox at work here too. We do not create union with the Divine or non-dual consciousness. We open up to it. We transform to realise it. It is already there, a truth of the nature of reality – it is already all one. As Dorothy in *The Wizard of Oz* learned when she wailed that she wanted to go home, the good witch, her loving guide, told her, "But you are home, all you have to do is wake up!" When we commit to the spiritual life we purge ourselves or are purged, sometimes gradually sometimes quickly, of all that gets in the way of this essential unity. In contemplation we come to union with the Beloved and thus are brought to the recognition (the re-cognition, the knowing again what we already know deep within) that separation was only ever a thought, a delusion, we were never really non-dual, it is and always was one.

Such a unitive consciousness, when we recover it, has many fruits for it informs every aspect of our being and doing in the world. This consciousness, free of ego agendas, is not neutral, but entirely loving and we bring this quality to our work, relationships and ourselves. The contemplative – as manager, doctor, nurse, teacher, shop worker, labourer, parent, friend, lover and on and on into every human role and endeavour – becomes a manifestation of loving awareness wherever we lead our lives. As servants and agents of change with this highest level of awareness, we become the compassionate Christ consciousness working in and through us in whatever we are engaged.

Purgation, illumination and union apply to many other aspects of our lives. We come to see the authenticity or otherwise of all the work and relationships in our lives when we are purged of our illusions, delusions and self-deceptions and awaken to what has heart and truth and meaning for us. This Way of purgation, illumination and union touches the way we respond to our spiritual practices across the spectrum from the reading of scripture to meditation and other Soul Works. We read and practice more deeply, constantly examining our understanding, intentions and expectations as our consciousness expands to reclaim its unitive condition. We may, for example, take a piece of inspirational writing and 'purge' our minds of initial impressions and interpretations to reveal new layers of meaning and possibility. We may pray dutifully, but ask, "Why am I doing this?" and thus purge ourselves of hidden, or maybe not so hidden agendas, such as the desire to appear more pure or spiritually committed than others. As I explored in *Coming Home*, the development of a healthy and integrated spiritual life requires the cultivation of ever deepening awareness, reflection and discernment.

The shift from an ego-centred worldview to one that is unitive, soul-centred, happens because the contemplative Way shines a light into the dark recesses of our consciousness. How can we not see differently when such a light flashes into our awareness? It is surely no coincidence that the origin of the word 'God' lies in the Sanskrit *Dyau* (meaning brilliance, illumination, day and light) and which in Greek becomes *Theos*. Seeing through to truth in this light not only draws us closer to the Beloved, but also to the world that is our home.

The 'drawing closer' into union does not turn us into otherworldly people detached from ordinary reality. It's one of the myths of the contemplative Way that we drop out from the 'real world'. Nothing could be further from the truth. Contemplation takes us deep within to the very core, the heart, of our being, but in doing so it enables us to engage with the world even more meaningfully and to participate in the healing of its brokenness.

Throughout the text I have mainly used the word 'God'; a loaded word if ever there was one and which you may recall I explored in detail in *Coming Home*. Suffice to say here that the term is used to give us a concept, a noun, to refer to that ineffable Absolute, the Divine, Ultimate Reality, the Nameless One, Sacred Unity, the Presence, the Beloved – so many names that can only hint at the profundity, intricacy and multi-form possibility of relationship of the One. Generations of humans have danced with concepts and nouns (just as I am doing now) to define this One in whom we live and move and have our being and who lives and moves and has being in us. Descriptions and definitions always for short, for this is the God that infuses all things yet is contained by none. This One is no separate idol or anthropomorphic entity standing outside of the ordinary reality of time and space. Yet, in eternity, the All-that-is is utterly not captured by them. Immanent and transcendent, personal and transpersonal, there are no limits to the unique way in which each one of us may come to the One. Thus, I have used names for God interchangeably throughout the text, on the understanding that they always fall short. In everyday life, I tend to settle upon the name Beloved, but please feel free to adopt a name, or none at all, that is most familiar and comfortable to you. Specifically I have sought to de-gender God in all my recent writings, a subject addressed in detail in *Coming Home*. God is referred to as 'He' and people as 'mankind' only where I quote original sources.

This unmanifest Beloved, this God, is beyond fully knowing, yet is nevertheless One whom we can sense, feel, relate to; One in whom we may experience ultimate intimacy, union. This numinous Being is simply the Love that loves to love, the very source of the creation itself, this vast work of art in which we are participants. This is a Oneness out of which everything comes and to which everything returns. As I write I am sitting in the great library at the Friary of St. Francis in Alnmouth in the North East of England, one of my favourite places of retreat. I have a grand view across the dunes and out to the glorious expanse of the North Sea. Around me, books are stacked from floor to ceiling, books ancient and modern oozing the delightful musty smell that only an old library can summon. Most of them point to the same thing, the timeless, relentless effort to say something about God. Theologians have tied themselves in knots, whole forests of trees have been felled for paper, billions of hours of labour expelled – all this to try and define what God is or wants or means. And I've just done the same in the few paragraphs above, it seems an inescapable human enterprise.

And yet, and yet...for the contemplative, theological debates become redundant, terms irrelevant. He or she moves beyond labels; the longing for God cancels out all obstructions, not least a gendered God or the limitations of words or the complexities of theology. The contemplative is less interested in knowing about the Beloved, more in being in and with. Out of this life-transforming relationship, the contemplative finds truth, love and our particular pathway of commitment and service.

The modern approach to theology has largely reduced it to an intellectual discourse on the truth or otherwise of dogma and doctrines, scripture and sacrament, often fixing God (the unfixable) into human definitions and reality. The mystics I have cited here offer a different and perhaps the original form of theology, that of the infinite possibility of Godly experience and relationship. Often we will read of their intense passion in this love and sometimes we can almost feel the struggle to get into words the rapture, wonder, love, sorrow and suffering they faced.

The language from some of these sources can also be quite challenging (to Christians, let alone to others!). For example, many early treatises on contemplation set great store on doing battle with bodily desires, sins and demons. With their archaic and seemingly bizarre or irrelevant language they can make grim and even incomprehensible reading to modern minds. Nowadays, with the benefits of psychology, we may see the inner struggle between good and evil more in terms of the tensions between our ego desires among the distractions of material reality and the heart's longing for connection, depth and meaning. Much of the early language also tends to be relentlessly masculine, yet paradoxically the contemplative Way has probably provided opportunities for more voices of women to be heard than any other branch of religious literature. One of these women, Mother Julian of Norwich in her "shewings" in the 14th century, challenged many as she described God not only as masculine but also as feminine – "Mother".

Jesus' teachings, either his own words or the words of those holy men and women inspired by him, are at the core of this book. If the language of some of these teachings is difficult, the situation is exacerbated by much of the debate about religion in our culture, particularly the often-warlike words and actions between different Christian factions. This book follows the thinking put forward in *Coming Home*; that most Christians are drawn to the spirituality of Jesus – a faith that is rooted in a longing for the experience of and relationship in the Divine, a wish to connect to others more deeply, to follow Jesus as he lived his life as supreme God-filled being, prophet of truth and social justice and an example, primarily through prayer, of consummate spiritual practice. Most Christians I encounter are far more interested in how they can live as Jesus did, full of compassion, wisdom and willingness to engage with the world to make it a better place and honour the creation, rather than getting distracted by reductionist theological debates about the truth or otherwise of various dogmas, religious rules or absolute interpretations of biblical stories.

Likewise, dear Unknown Friend, I believe most Christians long for an inclusive faith that says "you are welcome" rather than "you are welcome providing that ...you believe only what we believe or you are not gay or have extramarital sex or accept only our rules as true" or whatever other distinctions are used to create "otherness". The contemplative Way, as we shall see, is a path of union not separation, a way of maturing into a deep spirituality of connecting and relating. Indeed it may be argued that the solution to the present crisis in our churches lies in the deepening of the contemplative Way, transcending theological boundaries and reconnecting the church with the very heart of its purpose of helping people to get to God.

The early British church (now often called the 'Celtic' church) referred to the Bible as the 'little' book of God. That tradition also recognised the 'big' book of Creation - God present in the unfolding reality all around us, offering rich teachings to complement those we find in scripture. Jesus offers us some lessons here.

Firstly, he does indeed regularly refer to scripture (though often to challenge it) and we have at least one account of him reading in the synagogue from what we now call the Old Testament.

Secondly, he offers us the Book of Creation. Many of his stories and parables are peppered with examples (the lilies of the field, foxes with holes and so on) drawn from nature to illustrate his teachings.

Thirdly, there is the Book of Humanity. He offers many stories of the human experience (the sowers in the field, the prodigal son, the labourers in the vineyard) as well as the stories around him of the human encounter with him (the rich man, the centurion, the blind man, the haemorrhaging woman.). All of these present us with enriching examples of the human condition from which to learn; all the joys and struggles of seeking to follow the Way.

Lastly, there is the Book of the Heart, the way of contemplative prayer, the way of the mystic, the going within to that "inner chamber" [Matthew 6:6] where we open to a direct encounter with the Divine. Jesus prays regularly and gospel accounts tell of his search for solitude and silence. It is in the inner chamber that we come into the loving Presence in an intimate relationship, the soul opening to the divine splendour where we are inwardly transformed. That inner experience is not self-regarding, but works in us to change the way we live and act in the world following Jesus' teachings.

God is thus speaking to us not just in the written word, but also in the books of our interior and outer lives. Theological and moral insights are honoured and drawn upon, but contemplatives are less interested in seeking to reveal what God is, and more interested in letting God be revealed in ourselves. Theology invites us into exploration and belief *about* God; contemplation invites us into relationship and belief *in* God.

Perhaps a mark of our spiritual maturation, as I discussed in *Coming Home*, is a willingness to embrace the difficult, an ability to see through the fog of words and concepts that might alienate us to discover the essential truths that lie therein. In addition, there is a certain anti-intellectual bias in much of modern writing; spiritually complex ideas must be reduced to sound bites, quick fixes and the demands of a short attention span. This may be understandable when so many ancient writers express themselves in ways that no longer fit modern language, values and theologies. If some of the words are tough, please don't give up, but give attention, dear Unknown Friend!

In the spirit of "honouring thy father and thy mother", I have sought to acknowledge many of those who have influenced my thinking and practice down the years, who have inspired and encouraged. I hope you will experience the same. I have quoted these "mothers and fathers" both ancient and modern throughout the book. Each citation can be the substance of a spiritual exercise in its own right. Dear Unknown Friend, I invite you to pause when you come across such a quote, stay with it for a while and be open to the layers of meaning within. Our current view of the contemplative Way is so expansive because we stand on giants' shoulders. Generations of contemplatives have written about what we can encounter in the relationship with God - the dark nights of the senses or soul, illumination, rapture, the cloud of unknowing, ecstasy or agony; almost two thousand years of history are to be found here.

Our spiritual fathers and mothers mapped its joys and pitfalls and sometimes paid a heavy price, even with their lives, for daring to walk this Way against the laws and conventions of the time. Even today, the contemplative Way is still not universally accepted among the religious, as you will discover if you have not already. I regularly encounter participants in retreats or meditation meetings who say they have been "warned off" such inner work as "dangerous" or "an opening to Satan"; they attend with such warnings or carefully don't let others know of their interest.

Contemplatives from a mighty lineage speak to us in these pages, from John Cassian and the desert fathers and mothers of the first centuries of Christianity, to the medieval mystics such as Hildegard of Bingen and on to modern writers such as Simone Weil, David Torkington or Beverly Lanzetta. For those who wish to explore these and other works, I have included a full reading list at the end. Many would not be described as easy reading, but with patience and application the truths of which they speak can still shine through. In offering my own perspective, I suspect very little is new. Truth is eternal and unchanging, but has to be spoken in different ways to meet the needs of its time and place.

The modern spiritual supermarket is well stocked with tempting goods from all parts of the world, it can sometimes lead us to overlook the treasures on our own doorstep. The current trend to reduce food costs and carbon emissions is encouraging a return to consuming local foods wherever possible. Perhaps thinking and acting locally can also be applied to spiritual food. I have known people heaping ecstatic praise upon the writings of some new age guru pillaging oriental mysteries. Yet they are blissfully ignorant of the power of the works of Climacus, *The Cloud of Unknowing*, the *Philokalia*, van Ruysbroeck, Thomas Merton, Sister Wendy, John Main, Mother Julian and so many others. I recall being at a meeting of a group of Buddhism-seeking westerners in the presence of the Dalai Lama. He shocked many when he said that there was no need to go chasing Buddhism when what we seek might lie in our own tradition, right under our noses.

Furthermore, although I have quoted the writings of many well-known contemplatives, it is important to note that contemplation is for all. It is not just for special people who have had profound mystical experiences in special places and times or who pursued lives of extreme asceticism or religious devotion. Those who took the trouble to consign their thoughts to the page are easily outnumbered by the millions who did not. And it is worth remembering that in some eras those who did "go public" were often considered mad or were shunned or punished for implying that it is possible to know God by any way other than by obeying the rules of the day. Indeed many have died down the ages for suggesting that the path of the heart, simply loving God, is the only pre-requisite for awakening or "salvation", rather than adhering to certain doctrines or practices. We have the blessing of writings old and new to teach us now, often in language that is immensely rich and challenging, but that doesn't mean that what they experienced is only available to a rarefied few.

In some respects, the contemplative Way is right under our noses. It is, as we shall see, the path of descending with all our attention into the heart. It's not so much a Soul Work, a practice, rather it is a saying "Yes" to the Beloved, a giving of consent. To do so we have to show up, pay attention and do the preparatory work, such as meditation and prayer, then let go of any attachment to an outcome, to "getting something". Contemplation is not a skill (skill, if any, lies in the preparation) or something we acquire. It is a condition that may arise when we, having made ourselves available and waited, have allowed God to be God. Contemplation is the fruit of our courage, commitment and humility to do the work.

I hope the words and suggestions in this book will help you deepen your spiritual life and inform, illuminate and nourish an ever-greater opening of the heart to the Beloved.

With every blessing to you,

A Friend

February 2017

"Silence is the place where time and eternity embrace."
[Brother Raimon Panikkar 1918-2010]

Part 1

"But whenever you pray, go into your room and shut the door and pray to your Father who is in secret, and your Father who is in secret will reward you."
[Matthew 6:6 (NRSV)]

"When you want to lay yourself open to the divine...then go into your inner space to that story or that symbol that reminds you of the sacred. Close the doors of your awareness to the public person you think yourself to be. Pray to the parent of creation with your inner sense, the outer senses turned within. Veiling yourself, the mystery may be unveiled through you. By opening yourself to the flow of the sacred, somewhere, resounding in some inner form, the swell of the divine ocean can move through you. The breathing life of all reveals itself in the way you live your life."
[Matthew 6:6 (from the Aramaic translation by Neil Douglas-Klotz 1999)]

Introduction

The Cumbrian mountains rise up from the valley of my home. By the standards of mountains elsewhere they might be regarded as rather puny. Few of them are above a thousand metres and on a warm summer's day most look well rounded and inviting, suggesting a short stroll might be all it would take to reach the peaks and enjoy the views.

That impression is deceptive, for the paths are steep and often treacherous. Pleasant, warm sunshine in the valley may betray a climate ten or more degrees cooler on the tops. Weather patterns can change dramatically and you can begin your walk on a balmy day with not a breath of wind and within minutes cloud, cold and storm can sweep in. What seems like a sure path becomes lost in mist. Cliffs and ridges, so picturesque from below, are riven with unexpected gullies; sheer precipices plunge hundreds of feet. Wet rocks and worn tracks are not the sure foothold they appear from below. Unwary and ill-prepared walkers can quickly find themselves in serious trouble and each year many are lost and injured and some die. The number of casualties would be worse were it not for the work of dedicated and well-trained mountain rescue teams who are willing to be of service at all hours of day and night.

Walking the Lake District Fells, with all the attendant joys and risks, mirrors to some degree the pleasures and challenges of the spiritual life. A wise traveller on the Way sets out properly prepared - has map, compass, food and water for the journey and knows how and where to get help and advice both before and while en route. In *Coming Home* I looked closely at some of the prerequisites for safe spiritual awakening. Getting involved in spiritual practice is its own form of mountaineering (or perhaps a more appropriate metaphor is that of descending into deep caves) and in *Coming Home* I offered a guide, suggested routes and some thoughts on the best views. What follows is a deeper exploration of one of the ways to come Home: contemplation.

Millions of people have engaged in spiritual approaches (such as meditation, contemplation and prayer) handed down the generations for millennia. In the modern spiritual supermarket these terms have tended to be used loosely and often confusingly alongside visualisation, journeying or reflection, mainly to describe a shift in our consciousness out of the ordinary and everyday into the extra-ordinary encounter with inner stillness, the numinous, the Sacred Unity, God. Different understandings of these practices, especially from eastern and western spiritual traditions, have been mixed and matched, but not always successfully. The picture is muddied as many of these words have been taken up and debased in everyday language. We are asked, for example, to meditate upon a problem meaning to consider it and work it out. A moment's rest and introspection is considered to be contemplation. We pray for something in the sense of wish fulfilment.

Lots of courses and centres are available in the wild places of the world, like the Fells of Cumbria where I live, for those in search of the outward-bound adventure. The spiritual life is, initially at least, inward-bound, taking the Way of inner discovery and transformation from which place we also transform our way of being in the wider world. The contemplative Way is inward-bound adventure. Indeed, it is the route by which we discover our true self, our "I-Amness", stripping away all the delusions of who we think we are. It is also a Way by which we may find the Beloved:

"Contemplation...by which human beings are encouraged to open themselves to the penetrating Word/Spirit/Life of the Eternal, to rediscover their own Godlike nature, to be set free to live wisely, lovingly and powerfully."
[Peter Dodson and MartinTunnicliffe 2005]

Every religious tradition has mapped out numerous ways of getting to God, of becoming "enlightened" or finding bliss or nirvana. These approaches can be roughly divided into two dominant strands (which I have explored in more detail in *Coming Home*), although they often overlap. The first is the way of moralism. The seekers identify (or have identified for them) the elements of right conduct, which rules to follow, how to do good and be virtuous. Thus the seeker hopes to gain freedom from the shackles of ego consciousness (the little, lower or false self or the spell of "evil") and draw close to the Divine or secure salvation (however that may be seen) in this and/or the next life. For some Christians, for example, this might include following the Ten Commandments and the teachings of Jesus literally in order to avoid hell and ensure a place in heaven. Thus some traditions avoid, often because of fear, any way that is not about following the rules; they prefer to stay away from exploring the interior realm.

However, rules are notoriously open to interpretation and it is somewhat suspect if our faith is fear based - such a faith can be judgemental and damaging to ourselves and others. It can also be exhausting. In the effort to do good all the time we must draw upon our own resources, no matter how much we ask for God's help. It is especially draining if we do not feel like doing good. Any action we thus take is inauthentic; doing good may mask hostile feelings beneath. We feel worse, not better, as a result and our intentions end up being ineffective or distorted. If our hearts are not really "in it", any action we take risks being corrupted. Furthermore, all those unconscious, repressed feelings may be projected onto others not following "our" way– judging or attacking them.

However, it can be argued that such strenuous work may still indeed lead to a personal transformation and perhaps can inhibit some people from damaging others through a "good behaviour" template by which to live:

"The simple vision of truth ends in a movement of desire."
[St. Thomas Aquinas 1225-1274]

The second approach is the way of mysticism. This implies a relation to mystery, a tendency and desire of the human soul towards an intimate union with the Divine. It is a numinous and ineffable way and realised through contemplation and love. Authentic mysticism does not send us off into mysterious confusion, madness or an inability to function in the world. It draws us into a new relationship with the Beloved from which we are more able to engage with the world and with greater commitment and equanimity. This "movement of desire", as Thomas Aquinas put it, is love yet no ordinary love, for it is common in the language of contemplatives to describe it as burning, fiery and all-consuming as we will explore later. Contemplation is the mystic path to God, the encounter with an integrating knowledge and experience of the infinite. The seeker looks to transform consciousness and connect with God, to enter communion and union with the Divine.

Evelyn Underhill, in her classic text on mysticism, has explored the immense giving that is required to attain mystical union. All sense of personal agendas, efforts and thoughts of "who I am" or "what I want" have to be purged before we can be illuminated by truth and drawn completely into the unitive embrace of the Beloved. Entering mystical states may happen spontaneously to some people and many are cited in these pages. For most of us, however, it is a condition that has to be cultivated as we learn to set aside ego agendas and open ourselves to the inner transforming power of the Beloved.

The risks here are that the contemplative without proper guidance can become disconnected from ordinary reality, self-obsessed and disengaged from relationships with others and the world. The contemplative Way is also hard and demanding of discipline, but as the relationship to God deepens the inner transformation is set in train. Inwardly we can let go of the personal striving and energy consuming effort to do good. We learn instead to rest into being an expression of the Beloved's goodness at work in ourselves and through us in the world. If we are not careful, doing and being good by our own efforts can lead to a state of complete emotional, physical, mental and spiritual exhaustion; a subject I explore in detail in *Burnout*. The contemplative Way of inner transformation helps us to do good by first learning to be good through the compelling, transformative power of the Divine. In that sense, contemplation is not so much about the work that we do but about becoming receptive to God at work in us. It is a grace. Perhaps our part is to simply show up...and wait:

"The highest virtue of the soul is to know God...This virtue is the greater, the more the soul knows things by this method of knowing; thus he who can grasp things in this mode of knowing attains the highest human perfection. And consequently becomes filled with the highest joy, accompanied, moreover, by the conceptions of himself and of virtue. Thus there arises from this mode of knowing the highest peace of soul that is possible."
[Baruch de Spinoza 1632-1677]

Prayer, Meditation and Contemplation

These three terms are often used interchangeably, each has different meanings in different cultures and religious traditions and there is an enormous body of literature on all three subjects. Furthermore, prayer, meditation and, to some degree, contemplation have been subjected to extensive scientific research in recent years, especially in relation to health and wellbeing. On balance the studies point to general health and other benefits both for ourselves and for others (see also Wright and Sayre-Adams *Sacred Space* and Wright *Reflections* for more details) including:

Improved: capacity for intimacy with other people, personal energy, relaxation, psychological and cardiac stability, wound healing, healthy eating, exercise levels, posture, feeling a sense of control of one's life and being effective in the world.

Reduced: depression, fear of other people, sense of victimhood, smoking/alcohol consumption, substance misuse, anxiety, respiratory rate, pulse, blood pressure.

With such a long list of benefits attributed to these spiritual practices it could be asked why they are not available on prescription – although some doctors do prescribe them! Who wouldn't want to buy a product which offers so much yet at first glance seems to demand so little? All we need is a bit of time, no drugs and no special equipment. However, while these benefits are laudable, it has to be remembered from a spiritual perspective that the health gains from these practices are mere side-effects of the primary intention of seeking the Beloved.

I am often asked to teach meditation to help people cope with stress; it can be an impressive quick fix. But there is more to spiritual practice than seeking a kind of spiritual condom to protect us from the hazards of modern life. While they have much to commend them, meditation, prayer and contemplation have risks too. They can put us in touch with aspects of ourselves that are disturbing, even dangerous, if we are not properly guided and supported. While those who are experienced and have "done the work" can probably handle such challenges and trust in the help of the Divine therapist, those who have not can get into fierce difficulties. Unresolved wounds and fears can surface that may bring anxiety, depression or even psychosis. If we have unresolved neuroses, such as deep feelings of powerlessness, these can hook themselves onto our spiritual practice, for example turning powerlessness into controlling meditation groups or displays of superior experiences. Getting into spiritual work without undergoing the emotional work always leads to distortion of the former, as I explored in more detail in *Coming Home.*

Furthermore, in the case of prayer, not all prayers are positive. Some of the studies on prayer suggest it does indeed help and heal others, but some people pray for harm to come to others (see, for example, Larry Dossey's excellent exploration of the research on the effects of prayer). Does "negative prayer" have the opposite effect? And what does using negative prayer say about the person using it?

"...we can see why this first step is so difficult. No one willingly sees that he is not what he thinks and has always believed himself to be... spiritual exercises... begin by showing a man the first and, for some, the greatest obstacle in the path of self knowledge: the pain of seeing his own inner psychological disorder."
[Richard Temple 1960]

The risks of exposure to our "inner psychological disorder" are very real. Hence I advise caution with off-the-shelf guides to spiritual practices and I strongly recommend using this book within the context of the supportive approaches I have already outlined in *Coming Home*. Briefly, these entail pursuing spiritual exploration and practices (Soul Works) within the context of a Soul Community (a group of fellow travellers with whom we can share our encounters), the wisdom of tried and tested spiritual literature and other Soul Foods and access to one or more Soul Friends who can offer us wise spiritual direction. In this way we can better discern whether our inner experiences are valid and authentic and that body, mind and soul are taken care of when things get challenging. John Cassian relates the story of Hero, a keen penitent who lived alone for 50 years refusing all contact and advice. He eventually came to believe that all his ascetism had made him spiritually perfect, even to being able to defy the laws of nature. In rapture he leapt off a rocky ledge only to die. Without on-going guidance we can succumb to our delusions and ego inflations. Spiritual teachers of all kinds down the ages have emphasised the risks when the seeker loses grip on reality:

"For all spiritual questions it is necessary to have a director. The more extraordinary the ways by which the soul is led, the greater, as a rule, is the need for direction."
[Augustin Poulain 1836-1919]

In *Coming Home* I attached great importance to the need for spiritual direction along the Way. The bonds of the ego, of the ordinary life from which the seeker desires freedom, cannot be broken alone. In all traditions, not least the Christian, the experienced and authentic spiritual teacher, director or accompanier plays a pivotal role. Getting out of Egypt (in the Old Testament the place of slavery for the Hebrews and, symbolically in mystical literature, the landscape of material reality and ego entrapments that keeps the soul from God) as John Climacus reminds us, needs a guide:

"Those who wish to get away from Egypt, to escape from pharaoh, need some Moses to be our intermediary with God, to stand between action and contemplation...those who have given themselves up to God but imagine that they can go forward without a leader are surely deceiving themselves...we must have someone very skilled, a doctor, for our septic wounds...without we are...pitifully exposed to disaster."
[John Climacus c525-606]

So, if we have the necessary support in place for our escape from Egypt, we can set about engaging with our spiritual practice. Across all faiths, the three commonest are prayer, meditation and contemplation (although, as I have indicated at the beginning, it is questionable that contemplation is a 'practice', rather it is the preparation for it that is the work). What do these have in common and what are their differences? Unfortunately, the picture is far from clear. We can find references to petitionary and intercessionary prayer, meditative prayer, prayer, meditation, contemplation or contemplative prayer. Then there is Christian meditation – or Buddhist or Hindu or Sufi and so on. Often dictionaries and other sources overlap; definitions and interpretations of prayer, meditation and contemplation are used interchangeably and confusingly. What one person calls meditation may be contemplation to another, and on close scrutiny the difference between the two may be wafer thin. Everyday use of the words, as I suggested above, further confuses the picture.

For the purposes of this text I have rooted the discussion in the following understandings:

Prayer: The origins of the word lie in Middle English *preyen* and the Latin *precare*: to beg or ask earnestly. Prayer can be seen as the way we attempt to communicate with the Divine. We might do this because we want to offer worship or gratitude, seek help for another (intercessionary prayer), ask for help to change something (petitionary prayer) or confess our wrongdoings. In secular terms it may simply be an expression of hope or a heartfelt wish for something to happen. Prayer can be carried out silently, through words spoken or sung, individually or in groups and in stillness or movement such as circle dancing and body prayer. All the approaches with which we concern ourselves here involve inner stillness and may be practised in solitude or with others. Many of the authors I have cited use prayer to mean the foundation of contemplation and as the initial turning towards and entering into relationship with God. It is regarded by many as the keystone of the contemplative life:

"There is only one way to perfection and that is to pray. If anyone points to another direction, then they are deceiving you."
[St. Theresa of Avila 1515-1582]

Prayer is not just about asking God for things, it is the primary medium of relating to God. It requires us to prepare ourselves (it could be said that by simply picking up this book and reading it, at some level we are praying through our intention to seek and find the Divine), show up, pay attention and take action resulting from that relationship without attachment to outcome. It is not a passive silencing of our will and sitting there having fun, or otherwise, with God and then getting up and carrying on as normal. In the truest sense prayer is about opening to the transforming power of God, about how we are changed to act in the world.

Prayer, and the path of contemplation which it feeds, is not a relapse into self-gratification, passivity or apathy. It is revolutionary. It energises and calls us to connect with God and to work in the world; to participate in the creation even more fully as a result of what grows and empowers us in that relationship. Many ways of dropping out and escaping the controls and suffering of the world can be found in various traditions and spiritual practices both old and new. The contemplative Way compels us not to abandon the world but to play our part in the healing of it. It becomes a spur to social action, to care for the planet and all of creation. If through contemplation we discover the essence of God as holder and creator of all, in all and all in God, how could we not care for it and seek to act justly and compassionately? How, when we experience Divine love, can we not respond with love to all that has emanated from that loving Source?

This is the approach to prayer I have taken here, for this level of prayer is the root of contemplation; it is the exercising of spiritual muscle as a precursor to resting in the Divine before the work in the world that follows. This is not just for "special" people. Prayer is for everyone; it is proletarian. As St. Bonaventure reminds us, anyone can pray and grow through prayer:

> ***"And besides all this, if you would climb to the height of contemplation, and delight in the sweet embraces of the Bridegroom, exercise yourself in prayer, for this is the way by which the soul mounts up to contemplation and to the taste of heavenly things... You see, then, of how great virtue and power is prayer, and for proof of all that has been said (to say nothing of Holy Scripture) let this now be sufficient assurance that we have seen and heard, and see, day by day, many simple persons who have attained to all these things above mentioned and to others greater, through the exercise of prayer."***
> ***[St. Bonaventure c1221-1274]***

Brother Ramon, in the *The Flame of Sacred Love*, posits different qualities of maturity in prayer suggesting that we are "ankle deep" when using petitionary prayer. We go "knee deep" in intercessionary prayer and "waist deep" in the prayer of adoration. The prayer of contemplation is being "out of my depth". David Torkington (in *The Mystic*) offers a similar hierarchy of evolution in prayer. We mature from the "juvenile" level, where we talk to God like a Father Christmas, and on to "adult", where we connect more deeply with God, but still see the Divine as separate. Beyond this is the level of "perfect"; a state of integration or non-duality. It is to the latter that contemplation draws us.

Meditation: This is usually described as the discipline of quietening the relentless daily chatter in which the mind is engaged. We become still and calm with a sense of being fully present, attentive and in the moment. With its roots in the Latin *meditari* (to concentrate) and *medere* (to heal, to make whole) meditation suggests a condition of being in harmony through inner reflection and absence of distraction by thoughts or outer experiences, while at the same paying attention. Christian meditation tends towards the use of scripture or a story of Jesus or the repetition of a sacred word or words to go deep within so that greater meanings may be revealed. More recent books on Christian meditation seem to suggest a less distinct difference between that and contemplation. Oriental styles of meditation tend to emphasise the clearing and stilling of the mind, for example by repeating a word or phrase (*mantra*).

Sometimes if we have a problem or do not understand something we may be advised to meditate upon it, implying a goal-oriented sitting in silence. This illuminates one understanding of meditation as a kind of mental digestion, chewing over something until it is refined, broken down and understood. However, meditation with a purpose is an oxymoron. To meditate in this view is paradoxically to come to a place of purposelessness - simply to be, fully present, attentive and aware. Some traditions see the sense of being fully aware as an end in itself, others as a preparation for contemplation - the stilling of the mind and quietening of the distractions of ego identity being precursors to entering the "temple" that is contemplation.

"Meditation is a commitment to unity, and so it involves a turning away from alienation, from external divisions and from internal dividedness."
[John Main 1926-1982]

For Theresa of Avila, meditation was one of the "primitive" stages on the way to communion with the Divine. She likened it to drawing water up the well; it is hard work. After a while we get some help, being quiet and allowing God instead to do the work in us. Beyond is contemplative union, where God takes over completely. She saw the contemplative Way as not about emptying our minds to be filled with anything, but as a stage beyond meditation when the mental work is set down and the mind is quietened so that God can be heard. Our own exertions are left behind. The rest is up to God:

> ***"The life of prayer and contemplation is simply to realise God's presence in the depth of our being, in the depth of every being, and at the same time beyond all beings, beyond all that is within and without. It is certainly not a way life that is reserved for those few individuals who are specially called to escape from the world and take refuge in a desert. Contemplation and prayer are the very breath of life, not only for the true disciple of Jesus, but for everyone who has recognised his calling to be human."***
> ***[Abhishiktananda 1967]***

Two distinct stands of thought to prayer, meditation and contemplation thus begin to emerge. *Cataphatic* prayer (from the Greek *cata* - to descend, *phanai*- to speak; meaning to seek to draw God down into words, concepts, explanations) makes use of our faculties – memory, imagination, reason and thought. It is a function of the realm of our ordinary awareness and how we interpret the world through the five senses. It is the *via positiva* – the way of thought, action, concentration, effort. *Apophatic* prayer (from the Greek *apo* – other than/deny) is the *via negativa*. It bypasses our usual senses, lets them be set aside and gently rests in silence. There is no effort to conceptualise or 'do' something to get to God, rather to wait upon God, to "let God be God". It requires a willingness to be empty of our own desires, actions and thought processes and be open the possibility of going beyond the dualism of experience and experiencer, of God as separate from ourselves, of subject and object.

This *kenosis*, emptying of self in order to be receptive to Oneness in the

Self, might sound frightening to many. Indeed in some belief systems the emptying is seen as something to be avoided in case it creates a space for the devil. On the contrary, freed of the thinking and controlling mind, we become more receptive to the Divine, more possessed of it, not less. By emptying ourselves of our will we become more receptive to the Will. We see the ultimate expression of this in Jesus himself when his time of trial is imminent. In his prayers to God he asks, [Matthew 26:39] "Let this cup pass from me", but then he lets go of what he sees as his own will and surrenders into, "Not as I will, but as you will."

"Not my will, but Thine" are words found on my mother's grave, put there by my father in his grief many years ago. These words have been a prayer phrase or *mantra* that has rung in my consciousness for many a year.

Contemplation: We can find similarities to the contemplative way in most religious traditions. It emphasises a path to God rooted in the experience of relationship with God and, while this book has drawn on words from the Christian tradition, it is dependent on that relationship rather than adherent to the doctrines of a faith. It requires not so much theological or intellectual explorations, but more of what Plato called *nous* – the direct encounter, knowing and apprehension of God. Derived from the Latin *con templum* (to be with or in the temple, inner space/sanctum or holy of holies) the word contemplation suggests being in a place of completeness, "in the now" and seeing all. It is the "effortless effort" I described in *Coming Home*. It goes beyond the work, reflections and thinking involved in prayer or meditation. Arguably it is not work that we can do even if we try, but a gift of grace emanating from the Beloved rather than a goal achieved through our own actions. For contemplation is to be in a consciousness where we draw close to God, to let go of all our mantras, prayers, our efforts of listening, speaking and concentrating and so forth. Activity ceases. We become still and wait in a condition of consent, of "yes" to the Beloved. We wait, in faith, for the Beloved is the one who moves. By getting ourselves out of the way we open to the Presence of the One who has drawn us close.

In contemplation, we seek simply to be in the Presence, to let God be God, naked of all our expectations, occupations and imaginations. Many have tried to describe what it is to contemplate, but therein lies the paradox. We cannot know, through the intellectual processes of the mind, that which is ultimately unknowable. All reports, descriptions and accounts of experiences are attempts to conceptualise them and these mental efforts always fall short, albeit sometimes drawing very close in their portrayal. Some of the great mystical treatises such as those of Theresa of Avila or Julian of Norwich give us hints and clues. Poets like Eliot in *The Four Quartets* or composers like Taverner with *The Protecting Veil* or Tallis with the sublime *Spem in Alium*, may help us feel it. Yet its full representation is always ineffable, numinous, beyond the efforts of the thinking and word-bound mind:

"If you do not understand, I cannot help you. This is a miraculous work, of which one can tell you nothing, unless it is a lie."
[Marguerite Porete c13thC]

In the western Christian tradition a pattern of spiritual practice evolved known as *Lectio Divina* - divine or holy reading - encouraging the seeker towards contemplation. A passage of scripture would be chosen and the reader would dwell upon it in the following ways:

Lectio (reading) – reading repeatedly, staying with it and seeking layers of meaning and content, mining the text for its truths.

Meditatio (reflection) – allowing inner meanings to be explored and to sink in.

Oratio (reaction) – moving beyond facts/meanings and allowing the heart and mind to respond and rise to God.

Contemplatio (repose) – letting meanings, words or reactions pass away to be drawn into the loving gaze of God.

Reading sacred texts in this way allows us to go beyond surface meanings, develop spiritual *nous* and get past the literalism that bedevils many religious traditions.

It would have been alien to the Middle Eastern way of thinking to take scripture at face value, for it was considered to be food for the soul, to be savoured and digested slowly. Studying, interpreting and developing commentary on scripture like this, known in Hebrew as *midrash*, fostered illumination beyond literal interpretation and absolutes. Holy books do indeed contain literal, factual truth, but they also contain spiritual truth, which is not necessarily the same thing. For example, are the "enemies", the "wicked" or the "workers of evil" so frequently mentioned in the psalms just people attacking the pleading psalmist? Or are they expressions of the struggle of spiritual maturation – a spiritual truth about the battle with our ego attachments and the longing to be free of them?

When Jesus spoke in parables to help people understand the point he was trying to make he was not speaking literal truth. The audience listening to Jesus' teaching of the parable of the wicked tenants of the vineyard [Matthew 21: 33-46], for example, would not have asked, "Where was the vineyard" or "What was the name of the owner and how old was he?" The story is not about factual truth, but the spiritual truth of Divine generosity, trust, patience and justice.

The contemplative Way is the search for spiritual truth. By seeking to draw close to the truth of God beyond our surface impressions, interpretations and projections we hope for a relationship in God. Truth matters to a loving relationship. Clearing out anything that distorts or masks it helps a relationship to deepen, and contemplatives are lovers of truth and depth:

"Descend with your attention into the heart."
[St. Theophan, the Recluse 1815-1894]

Lectio divina and our preparations for prayer help us to step deeper into the truth of God, but the process is rarely linear. It is one of comings and goings rather than a series of "stages", although with some apparently identifiable phases. Some attempts have been made to set out contemplation in a similar way. For example, we may spend some time in concentration – getting ourselves ready, paying attention to our posture, comfort, environment, reading something inspiring or seeking the right words for a prayer or *mantra*. We may then find ourselves praying, talking to God, making requests and repeating prayer words that have a heartfelt meaning for us. Then we may slip into a meditative state, where either the prayer or holding a particular image or repeating a word or series of words (which may themselves be a prayer) quiets the mind and helps us let go of our agendas and interior or exterior distractions.

In this aware in-the-moment space, we wait. It is a waiting emptied of our wishes or needs. In the waiting we may discern something that at first may seem quite startling – that this awareness is not neutral. This *enstasis*, pure awareness, has an entirely loving quality to it – from the still point within we may "see" ourselves with complete compassion for all our struggles in life (rather than giving way to the relentless voice of the inner critic that tells us we are not good, loved or worthy). We may discern that this 'seeing' is mirrored in the gaze of the Beloved with the same compassion. Here we may know the boundless love that dances between the gaze of lover and Beloved, Bridegroom and Bride…a "nowness" that is utterly loving where all words and concepts, definitions of seeing, gazing, separateness, time and place fall away. Many report this quality of the waiting space, this liminal space that is both full and empty, knowing and unknowing.

I have explored waiting, in the spiritual sense, in *Coming Home*. The waiting in contemplation is not like hanging around in a queue with thoughts of anticipation, desire or or expectation. Being aware of all these the contemplative lets them be emptied out and simply remains present, ready to be drawn ever more deeply into the presence of the Divine, to be immersed in that love where we are both lost and found, in that place that is no place, where we know and do not know, where we see and do not see, where we hear and do not hear. It is the place of darkness, not of evil, but the luminous darkness of the Divine, a light so bright that we cannot see, where the power of the ego is dissolved; the inexpressible darkness of the known yet unknown. This is the *gnophos* , the dark cloud of the unknowable God [Ex. 20:21], where we may be transported beyond ordinary perceptions of self, reality and God that cannot easily be put into words. In this altered state of consciousness, arguably the highest consciousness, we are profoundly aware, silent, wordless, gazing at God as God gazes upon us; thus there is only one gaze:

> ***"A never to be ended give-and-take is set up between the individual and the Absolute. The spirit of life has been born: and the first word it learns to say is Abba, Father. It aspires to its origin, to Life in its most intense manifestation…it knows itself a member of that mighty family in which the stars are numbered: the family of the sons of God who, free and creative, sharing the rapture of a living, striving Cosmos, shout for joy."***
> ***[Evelyn Underhill 1875-1941]***

In contemplation we listen for God, open ourselves to God and wait silently upon God. We look to be aware of the presence of God, being quiet and attentive in that Presence, open to what it is that God seeks to work in us. Words of prayer may begin this attentiveness and some examples will be given later, but in the end they may just get in the way. The contemplative learns to put words down, and simply be with God.

Contemplation and mysticism are closely related. The mystic may plunge spontaneously into a sense of communion with the Divine, but as Evelyn Underhill has pointed out in her brilliant thesis on mysticism, contemplation is the "mechanism of the mystic." She sees concentration of intention upon the "object of desire" as an essential precursor to contemplation. It is the "psychic gateway" - a method of going from one level of consciousness to another, "the condition under which he shifts his field of perception and obtains his characteristic outlook on the universe". Another sense of consciousness is liberated beyond the normal powers of the mind, through which the creation and the Divine are seen anew and once tasted the world and the perception of and participation in it are never the same again. The experience brings the contemplative into a new relationship with "ordinary reality", an awareness beyond explanation and reason.

The mystic-contemplative passes beyond the frames of reference of ordinary seeing and sees instead through what Saint Augustine called the "mysterious eye of the soul" into "the light that never changes". It is the power of seeing into eternity, which is not "forever", not a condition in time and space, but a "nowness" in which all time and space is contained.

The true contemplative does not seek mystic delights, insight or wisdom, though these are the fruits of the spirit as we will explore later. Rather we contemplate because we can do no other; we go where we must for the sake of love. We may recognise those ego drives in ourselves for achievement or pay-offs or comforts, but we let these be or let them go. No reward is expected. The journey to God leads to the journey in God. Many stages are described in different traditions but all emphasise a gradual raising of consciousness, a drawing closer through emptying of ego attachments and illusions into the deepest truth. By transcending and escaping the limitations of ego consciousness, the contemplative expands consciousness and opens to the infinite. Prayer words are the raft on which the contemplative sails, only to leave this raft behind to float free in the ocean of consciousness, of Divine love.

Reflection upon our own insignificance is part of this process, for it aids surrender into a greater realm of being. Yet, paradoxically, through this we discover our true specialness. We are indeed insignificant humans in the face of the vastness of the universe and the power of the Absolute, but it is this vastness that makes us significant; we are each unique. No one will ever look through our eyes and know the world and the stars beyond as we do, uniquely, during our lives. This is how special we are, in all of the creation, as far as we know, we are each of us "one-offs". Each microsecond is unique and uniquely seen by us. In some traditions it is believed that the Beloved created humanity so that the GodSelf might be seen reflected unto itself. Thus through each life God sees God mirrored back in the infinite possibility of the creation, never before and never again in exactly the same way.

Spiritual "marriage" is the hope of the contemplative. The soul is the bride; the Divine is the Bridegroom. Descriptions in the literature are rich with this recurring theme as we shall see later, yet this game of love is rarely linear. Like all relationships it is full of flux, of knowing and not knowing, togetherness and separation, connection and disconnection. With attention the fluctuations diminish; there is a gradual maturing and merging beyond "states". The mystic marriage is the fulfilling union of the soul with its source. This is not a loss of life or individuality, but gain. Through this marriage the contemplative is energised to live an intense and creative life within the temporal order in communion with the Absolute. The contemplative lives as never before, infused with the vitality of the unquenchable source of life itself.

The struggle to attain this vitality is not one of denial or punishment, but the integration of the authority of the soul, the source of life, in our lives. Spiritual exercises are needed to support this and among these, arguably the supreme exercise, is contemplation. Much of the literature on the subject may appear alien to modern sensibilities (see, for example, the "satanic" language of St. Bonaventure). Nowadays we are more likely to speak of wrestling the power of the ego away from the soul, so that it may unite with its creator. Although beliefs on this subject may differ, the essential process is the same:

"God alone can give consolation to the soul without any previous cause. It belongs solely to the Creator to come into the soul, to leave it, to act upon it, to draw it wholly to the love of His Divine Majesty. I said without previous cause, that is, without any preceding perception or knowledge of any subject by which a soul might be led to such a consolation through its own acts of intellect and will."
[St. Ignatius of Loyola 1491-1556]

The contemplative has often been seen as someone special, holed up in a religious community. But the contemporary world, as I have suggested in *Coming Home*, is full of opportunities for participating in a religious tradition and community, of seeking spiritual support that transcends historical patterns of organisation. The contemporary contemplative exists like a "new monastic" (see *Coming Home* and McEntee and Bucko's *New Monasticism*, the latter being deeply influenced by the contemplative tradition) beyond the dualism of the "spiritual" life and "ordinary" life, integrating these perceptions into a whole to live fully in the world:

"To say it briefly, prayer becomes something you are, not something you do. Your life and consciousness become the channel through which the meaning of God flows into human life. Prayer becomes the activity of opening your life to this deeper presence, this transcendent power we call God. Petition becomes the way you share life and love with others. Intercession becomes your willingness to be involved in causes of justice that help to build a world in which all people can live fully, love wastefully and be all they can be. Thanksgiving becomes the constant awareness of the way God changes lives. Meditation and contemplation become the means of spiritual growth and the development of a God consciousness and the praying person becomes deeply aware that God works through his or her life constantly."
[John Shelby Spong 2010]

Thus, as we mature in the contemplative Way, there is no time of not contemplating; the change of consciousness towards the non-dual is such that contemplation has become a way of life. We become a living prayer, engaged fully in life while always at Home in the Divine. It is worth remembering, as explored in *Coming Home*, that Home is not a static place in the sense of stuckness or absence from all the movement or turbulence in the world (or in ourselves). We are always coming Home; there is never an end point. And Home, like our own homes, is also a place of change at some level. Yet the Home we refer to here is that place of consciousness and awareness, a condition of being still within movement, of repose within activity; an inner stillness out of which clear, aware, truthful, compassionate and insightful action emerges. It is to be "in the temple" while cognisant of the world in which the temple rests. To be "in the temple" without duality is perhaps bringing to fruition the meaning of:

"Pray without ceasing"
[Thessalonians 5:17]

Prayer for the contemplative moves beyond "an order of words", as Eliot put it, a mere conversation between separate lovers, an activity at set times. Contemplation purifies us of duality, of perceptions of praying or not praying, of our ego distinctions and separateness. In sinking more deeply into God we lose our individuality only to find our true individuality, the soul, our perfect unique soul. We manifest in the world with less and less ego clutter as time goes by. The power of silence takes us deep into a noiseless place that it is integrated into everyday life. No matter what thoughts or actions engage us or whatever movement is taking place in the world, in the interior realm the contemplative is still and silent in God. All the work of concentration, prayer and meditation is put down. The soul enters its Sabbath time, resting attentively without concentration in God, perfectly still yet moving in all the glory of the Divine consciousness that is revealed to us, deeply ignorant yet profoundly aware in the infinity of All-that-is. Life itself, our own life, has become a prayer.

This is no grandiose, ego-inflated state. In knowing, we encounter a deep humility, the profundity of not knowing. We see how we are feathers "on the breath of God" as Hildegard of Bingen observed. Such immersion in the unity of Divine will is echoed by de Chardin:

"It is in no way metaphorical to say that man finds himself capable of experiencing and discovering his God in the whole length, breadth and depth of the world in movement. To be able to say literally to God that one loves Him with, not only with all one's body, all one's heart and all one's soul, but with every fibre of the unifying universe – that is a prayer that can only be made in space-time." [Teilhard de Chardin 1881-1955 (The Phenomenon of Man)]

The prayer of contemplation exposes the redundancy of concepts of "this" world or "that" world, until there is no this or that any longer, but One.

Contemplation and Mindfulness

In recent years there has been a huge expansion of interest in mindfulness. I am often asked in classes if contemplation is the same thing. It is related as a way of interior exploration, cultivating awareness and quietening of the mind with its attendant health benefits as mentioned above.

A little-known meeting took place in Downing Street, the home of the UK's prime minister, in 2013 when John Kabat-Zinn was invited to give his advice. He is Professor of Medicine Emeritus and founding director of the Stress Reduction Clinic and the Center for Mindfulness in Medicine, Health Care, and Society at the University of Massachusetts Medical School.

In an article by Madeleine Bunting in the Guardian newspaper that April, tellingly titled *Zen and the art of keeping the NHS bill under control* he said "Mindfulness has unlimited applicability to almost every health care issue we now face – and it's cheap." He noted that the evidence for its beneficial effects upon stress, hypertension, anxiety and cancer is strong. Mindfulness is often associated and promoted with another fashionable buzzword 'resilience'. Building resilience, a person's ability to survive in difficult times and in stressful workplaces, would seem self-evidently good.

However, there may be a risk here of debasing and distorting a very powerful spiritual practice. Much of the current promotion of mindfulness (apart from making a lot of money for some individuals and organisations) seems to buy into the zeitgeist that "it's all down to you" – that whatever is going wrong in life and work is the result of our own moral or other weaknesses that we can put right with a bit of work. Thus, stressed people get asked, "What's wrong with you?" rather than, "What's wrong with the circumstances that have made you stressed?" Responsibilities (and costs) of making sure the setting has the right resources may be bypassed if all manner of health and social problems can be put down to individual failings. Many of the resilience building/mindfulness website and self-help tools are breathtaking in their lack of attention to the responsibilities of communities, governments and organisations.

Mindfulness, like contemplation, is not value-free and cannot be divorced from its underlying Buddhist philosophy, not least what "mind" is, whether God is a reality or the nature of non-attachment. The marketers of mindfulness do not always seem to be candid about this and its implications.

Mindfulness is a spiritual practice of profound implications for healing and personal transformation. Reducing it to a cure-all stress reduction/self preservation technique seems to devalue it; these are side effects of mindfulness, not its core intent. Using mindfulness to medicate life's pain can easily confuse non-attachment with detachment without careful teaching (they are not the same). The former helps us to be in the world and to act with compassion while not getting sucked into stress and burnout, the latter is a way of cutting off from things as a defence mechanism. Authentic spiritual practice is not a way of avoiding the suffering in the world but of engaging with it more deeply and safely. Without care, mindfulness becomes just another way of keeping people quiet instead of an encouragement to question and challenge.

Embracing oriental mindfulness may lead us to ignore indigenous options, as the comment from the Dalai Lama, which I mentioned at the beginning of this book, illustrates. The rich tradition of the Christian meditative and contemplative ways is replete with health benefits and cultivating loving awareness. The different philosophical roots also hold the possibility that there is

"Something Other" available to help us...we are not on our own. It may be that we are not always clear about the underlying drives to choose mindfulness – is it seen as a soft option, is it buying into popularity for the sake of it, is it a way of avoiding the grittier work of confronting our fears or woundedness around Christianity?

Although often used interchangeably, mindfulness and awareness are not necessarily the same. The former, to some, is a means of developing the 'witness' in our consciousness. It is often assumed to have a neutral 'observer' quality to it that can keep us separate from the pain of the world – a seductive quality sometimes used to market it. The contemplative tradition and lineage sees the cultivation of awareness as a primary focus of inner work, but it is not a neutral awareness, rather a loving one, a quality of consciousness that awakens the heart to fully engage in the pain and joy of the world. It encourages compassionate action, but, to quote Krishna in the *Baghavad Gita*, "with peace in your heart" so that we do not exhaust ourselves and burn out. The contemplative Way summons us within, but then urges us outward from a place of equanimity to embrace and participate in the world of suffering.

Preparing the Way

If the journey into contemplation is ultimately opening to God, the Source-of-All, the very ground of our being then it is a serious undertaking. Preparation is needed in the early stages as we learn to expand our consciousness and go deeper and deeper. Here are some suggestions to aid the practice, but let me reiterate that I recommend they are followed under the guidance of a supportive Soul Friend and Soul Community. While to some degree we can trust that we will be safe and taken care of in our seeking, many disturbing things can occur in spiritual work and we need the holding and guidance of others. Indeed a fruit of spiritual maturation is a willingness to engage with others, to have the humility that we do not have all the answers and the awareness that some practices are so demanding that we must be able and willing to access the authority of others.

For prayer to become a way of life, the discipline of regular practice is needed until we find a pattern that works for us. There may come a time when the boundaries between practising and not practising become less and less distinct:

> ***"If all goes well, the prayer that starts and develops at set times ought to spread out gradually and filter through the rest of the day. In the end, it will become coextensive with all and everything we do. To begin with, the prayer period will be like a desert: dry, arid and barren. But it will eventually become an oasis in our lives that we cannot do without. However, that's not the end, it's only the beginning. In the end, the oasis will become a fountain that will well up and brim over to irrigate the whole of our lives."***
> ***[David Torkington 1999 (The Hermit)]***

Almost every commentary on prayer, meditation or contemplation offers tips on preparation. The common ground is the need to become relaxed, aware and free of distractions, to become quieted in every sense so that we may be fully open to the Presence. Many of us in the maelstrom of ordinary life can find it very difficult to find quiet time and it can be hard to engage with that quietness when the mind seems to be pulling in every direction. So, whether you already have a practice for becoming still and quiet or whether you are new to contemplation, consider the following simple relaxation exercise to help cultivate inner calm and receptivity:

1. Find a quiet place where you can be free from interruptions. Make sure you have the time set aside just to devote to practice. Some people get concerned that they may fall into a relaxed state and fall asleep or not "come back" in time for an appointment. It is surprising how quickly our own body clock seems to take over reliably. All the same, make the space as free as possible from the feeling of being "timetabled". Make the setting as pleasant as you wish if it's your own room – light a candle, dim the lights, add flowers and so on to create an environment that is aesthetically pleasing to you

and in which you might include religious rituals, symbols and scripture that are important to you. If possible, perhaps you can set aside a special place and/or time at home or work that is just dedicated to silence and stillness. If outdoors, find a pleasant place in nature, by a tree, a garden – whatever pleases you. With practice you may find that these requirements pass away and you will be able to practise anywhere. In the meantime, the way we prepare ourselves – going to a particular place, meeting certain people, reading inspirational texts, lighting a candle and so on can all be part of our conscious "pilgrimage", the steps along the way as we shift our consciousness and intention to being committed to resting in our deepest Self.

2. Get comfortable in a chair, on a cushion or meditation stool – avoid lying down as you may just fall asleep. Sit and check your body posture for comfort, close your eyes and check your body from head to toe that it feels relaxed. If necessary, move, tighten and relax the muscles and limbs that are tense. For the contemplative, no special posture is needed other than that which allows both comfort and attention. You do not have to cross your legs in the lotus position, prostrate yourself, kneel down or adopt any other position for that matter. You can do so if you wish, if you find such positioning conducive, but there is no requirement. Just allow yourself to be comfortable. Personally, I find that sitting cross legged on the floor with good back support is all that is needed, or in a chair following the "90 degrees" rule – the head, neck and spine upright and in alignment but gently and not rigidly so, and, with the bottom in the seat corner, making a 90 degree angle with the thighs. The knees should be bent to make an angle of about 90 degrees. with thighs and lower legs, then the feet flat on the floor at 90 deg. to the legs. The arms are relaxed with the palms resting on the knees or facing upwards.

3. Then, keeping your eyes closed, bring your attention to the place where you are sitting. Feel the air temperature; listen to the background sounds and smells. Just become aware of your environment. If you are not comfortable sitting with your eyes closed then leave them open but focus on a

nearby object such as a candle in front of you. Let your gaze stay with that for a little while or simply look downwards at the floor and let your gaze go out of focus.

4. Now bring your attention back into your body and check comfort once more. Feel yourself just sitting there, the position of your body, the solidness of it in the chair or on a cushion, the ground beneath you and the contact of clothing with skin; very safe and solid and present in the world.

5. Gradually, as you sit there, bring your attention from your body and into your normal breathing for a minute. Then take a big stretching breath, the biggest you can with a pause between the in-breath and out-breath. Do this twice more. Then relax into normal breathing.

6. Now count the out-breaths, one to four as you breathe out in sequence. Just keep doing this for as long as you wish. When you have counted four breaths, count the next four again from one until four – repeat the cycle continuously.

7. Notice distracting thoughts – and as soon as you do, gently bring yourself back to counting. Know that all you have to do is count and breathe. Just sit and allow yourself to relax into it, watching your thoughts come and go and the tricks of the mind trying to pull you away, such as setting strict goals and expectations of what you want to happen. These can keep us stuck - your desire for things to happen or not happen gets in the way of them happening! So, just learn to relax and sit – and let the rest take its course. Don't try and force out distractions, they only get stronger if you do so. It's as if they are fed by the energy put into trying to get rid of them. As soon as you become aware that your attention has drifted, gently ease yourself back to counting, just prefer it and don't force it – this is gentle attention not concentration with effort. Watch out for all those punishing thoughts "I'm no good at it", "I keep forgetting", "It's boring" etc. etc. These are just thoughts like any other, they

have no power of their own except what you choose to give them. As soon as you notice you are distracted, gently ease yourself back into the breathing and counting. No matter how interesting the thoughts let them go and come back to counting. In time you will find you are distracted less and less, and you come to simply sit at ease more and more, just "aware".

8. If you notice distractions in the room or beyond, as before, do not try to force them out, just absorb them with ease, make them part of the sitting. Forcing only makes them more irritating. Feeling sleepy? Most people do when they begin – there is no complex spiritual reason for this and you are not "no good at it" you are simply tired! Use this information – do you need to have a nap? If so, do so and then come back to the exercise afterwards. Perhaps you need to rethink your sleep and work patterns to promote more rest and/or look at sitting at times of day when you feel more refreshed and awake (e.g. first thing in the morning).

9. As you feel ready to finish, let go of the counting and pay attention to your normal breathing for a moment. Just sit for a little while more and allow yourself to experience the stillness and sense of just being aware and in the moment. Take a deep breath again and as you breathe out this time bring your attention back into your body; feel yourself sitting on the chair, your feet on the ground, the contact of clothing with skin, the body very solid and present in the world. Take a deep breath once more and this time bring your attention from your body back into your environment, but keep your eyes closed; feel, smell and listen to the place you are in once more. Then breathe deeply again and this time, as you breathe out, slowly open your eyes, looking downwards first. Move gently and come back into the world – take your time. Rest or sleep more if you need to.

10. Regardless of whether you develop this exercise into prayer or as an end in itself, regular practice will bring many health benefits. I recommend doing this at least once or twice a day, more if you can and for as long as you can, at least 5

minutes – even a little is better than none at all. Start off with short episodes first so you do not make it too difficult for yourself. Setting yourself up to be perfect just disappoints and demotivates if you don't achieve a "goal". For some people this time of relaxation is enough. Others, however, having learned to be still and quiet, find this has been useful practice before prayer, meditation or contemplation. After a while you may build up to, say, an hour a day or longer. You can use this simple technique at any time during the day if you need a break or feel stressed. Use the breath, especially the stretching breaths to calm you if you feel you are becoming tense but aren't in a place where you can withdraw for a moment. You'll be surprised at how you can seemingly carry on normal conversation and no one notices that your attention has also moved to your breathing at the same time.

Simple breath-work and relaxation techniques like this can help us learn to be still and develop confidence in our ability to open to deeper levels of prayer, meditation and contemplation. (Some of the prayer suggestions at the end of this book can be accompanied by attention to the inward/outward flow of the breath, as will be explained later). The sense of stillness and being fully present in the here and now that can arises from such practices are beneficial to our health and wellbeing as I suggested earlier, and for many people this is sufficient. Some may find similar experiences arise in movement, such as body prayer or tai chi, with a particular hobby or pastime that absorbs all of our attention, or during sports such as cycling, swimming or hill walking. Some may realise there is more to it than a general sense of wellbeing and peace; a transcendent quality emerges, a sense of connection to the Divine, mystical experiences, expansive states of consciousness. To be "spiritual" in this way is much more common than is realised or is acknowledged in our very materialist world. The Alister Hardy Trust, currently based at the University of Wales at Lampeter, has spent many decades documenting the religious, transcendent or numinous experience of thousands of people. Despite the strong sceptical discourse in our culture, it seems that most people persist in experiencing them. On this basis numinous experiences are not abnormal, to not have them is abnormal!

With practice and discipline, and yes it does take both, we can find that it becomes easier and easier to slip into a relaxed state of preparation. Others find that a brief flicker of inner quiet attention is all that is needed. What does seem to matter for most of us, however, is consistent attention, perhaps daily or twice daily or more of quietness and sinking into stillness.

Abbot Anthony, one of the earliest documented desert fathers, saw how the busy world can suck us into it. Even the most committed seekers can find themselves falling into distraction and losing attention to their inner life. Coming back into our "cell", our quiet inner space, is part of the discipline of serious spirituality:

"Just as fish die if they remain on dry land so monks, remaining away from their cells, or dwelling with men of the world, lose their determination to persevere in solitary prayer. Therefore, just as the fish should go back to the sea, so we must return to our cells, lest remaining outside we forget to watch over ourselves interiorly."
[Abbot Anthony 251-256]

For most of us, a lot of groundwork has to be done so that we become contemplative and enter a condition of "prayer without ceasing". This can include, especially in the early days, working with our Soul Friend to see what teachings lie in the inner experiences and learning to stay with the commitment to regular practice. A lot of undoing of old habits and the healing of old wounds may be needed, not to mention the sheer effort of commitment when other temptations may offer powerful seductions away from the inner life. We can feel like we are really deprived and suffering at such times. Just like the addict gets withdrawal symptoms from heroin, so our addictions to the ego driven life (longings for power, control, pleasure, security) have an equally strong attraction:

"...by means of this dim contemplation, in which the soul is made to suffer from the failure and withdrawal of its natural powers, which is a most distressing pain. It is like that of a person being suffocated, or hindered from breathing. But this contemplation is also purifying the soul, undoing or emptying it, or consuming in it, as fire consumes the rust and mouldiness of metal, all the affections and habits of imperfection which it has contracted in the whole course of its life."
[St. John of the Cross 1542-1591 (The Dark Night of the Soul)]

The thought that we might have to work for the spiritual life can itself be off-putting. It may become another ego excuse for not bothering. For most of us with busy lives the possibility of having more demands placed upon us may be the last thing we need. However, our efforts can be reinforced when we notice that there is also much joy and release to be found as well. And it is important to remember, as St. John of the Cross says, that the struggles are invariably precursors to the soul drawing closer to God.

"We see nothing, we walk gropingly, and ... ordinarily things do not come about as they have been foreseen and advised. One falls and, just when one thinks oneself at the bottom of an abyss, one finds oneself on one's feet."
[Marie de l'Incarnation 1599-1672]

Nevertheless, the contemplative Way is not for the faint-hearted or those who prefer the superficial life. There is nothing essentially complicated or difficult about contemplation itself, but it does require commitment, patience, persistence and perseverance and a willingness to pay attention to those inner promptings that long for God. Contemplation is less about us doing the work to get to God and more about us doing the work to get out of the way so that God can be at work in us.

"The real difficulty about prayer is that it has no difficulty. Prayer is God's taking possession of us. We expose to Him who we are, and He gazes on us with the creative eye of Holy Love. His gaze is transforming: He does not leave us in our poverty but draws us into being all we are meant to become. What this is we can never know. Total Love sees us in total truth because it is only He who sees us totally."
[Sister Wendy Becket 1994]

Coming to that place of deep trust and working through the many spiritual and psychological encrustations that obscure the gaze of "the creative eye of Holy Love" is the stuff of inner labour. In my view, it's the hardest work we can ever do. That is why so many shy away from it. Perhaps we lack the spiritual stamina to dig deeply. Maybe it is easier to stay light and fluffy and seek only pleasant experiences. Perhaps we would rather avoid the pain that comes when we do not like what we see within and fear that we are unable to transform it. Or maybe it is the anxiety of realising in contemplation that we are fully seen and known whatever our will. Yet, as Thomas Merton reminds us, that anxiety is lost when we realise that in being fully known we are also fully loved, no matter what flaws we seem to have. In losing concern for ourselves, we find a loving concern that is infinitely beyond the self:

"... if we consider the joy of mystical union abstractly, merely as something which perfects our own being and gives us the highest possible happiness and satisfaction, it is possible to desire it with a desire that is selfish and full of pride. And this pride will be all the greater if our desire implies that this consummation is somehow due to us, as if we had a right to it, as if there were something we could do to earn it for ourselves. This is the way mystical union appears in the minds of those who have no idea what it really is. They do not realise that the essence of that union is pure and selfless love that empties the soul of all pride and all attachment to its own will and its own judgement, and annihilates it in the sight of God in order that nothing may be left of it but the pure capacity for Him. If you do not clearly understand that the joy of the mystical love of God springs from a liberation from all pride, you cannot desire it as it ought to be desired...for the only way to enter that joy is to dwindle down to a vanishing point and become absorbed in God through the centre of your own nothingness."
[Thomas Merton 1915-1968 (Seeds of Contemplation)]

The contemplative Way is therefore not about giving us lots of exciting experiences or ego feel-good factors. Much of New Age spirituality, indeed quite a lot of Old Age spirituality, tends to focus on the search for the spiritual "highs". The contemplative has no interest in such ephemera, but longs for depth. To do so carries the hope, the trust, that the light of the Divine is real, is present within.

"Faith that the divine light is present within us – a conviction not necessarily an experience – is the primary foundation."
[Father Thomas Keating 1994]

This "foundation" nurtures the conscious desire to come to the Beloved directly and unmediated, to fulfil the heart's longing for that reunion, a longing that everyone feels at some level, but denied by egoic addictions of acquisitiveness, busyness, shopping, serial relationships, drugs and others as I explored more thoroughly in *Coming Home*. In short it is the most important commitment we can make, for it is a commitment to the Ultimate, the Absolute, God. This is serious business and while it is to be undertaken joyfully and with a lightness of touch, it also demands dilligence, discipline and an appreciation of the depths to which we are invited:

> ***"I do not want to give an impression of glibness in talking about familiarity with God in prayer. It does indeed happen that we become intimate with God in prayer, but in the process we do not lose the sense of God's greatness, his infinity. He remains GOD, the ineffable creator who 'dwells in inaccessible light' and cannot be grasped by the human mind because he is too far above it. In other words, alongside the growth of familiarity with God in contemplation there also grows a corresponding awe that this should be."***
> ***[John Dalrymple 1984]***

My role as an interfaith minister brings me into contact each year with students who are following the programme at the OneSpirit Interfaith Seminary. As their spiritual director or supervisor I work closely with them until the day of ordination dawns. On that day they have to take the communal vow of service, a promise to God, which all ministers must make, but they are also required to write and commit their own personal vow. One thing they have to face up to is the importance of that vow or perhaps, more accurately, to whom it is being made. I am often reminded of how my fellow students and I in the run up to our own ordination experienced high anxiety of all sorts. Mine was a recurring dream, or nightmare; I was on a train, the only passenger and there was no driver. And there were no railway lines. The train was hurtling at immense and accelerating speed towards a cliff, beyond which there was a vast fall into nothingness. The dream came every few months, then every few weeks, then every night in the last days before the ceremony.

An analyst could no doubt have a field day with such a dream, but the story here makes the point that in committing to our relationship to God all kinds of fears, conscious and unconscious, will be at play as we draw closer and make promises to the Divine. When we think about it such a promise, while rooted in the love of God, carries with it all kinds of undercurrents of human fear. Of course the ego, the very bastion of personal and worldly power, does all it can to avoid that kind of surrender. It wants to stay quite firmly in charge and is terrified of annihilation. Thus the contemplative Way draws us into the love of God, but to a greater or lesser extent this brings with it some degree of apprehension. This is the grist to the mill of the work with the spiritual director:

"Our prayer must be humble, fervent, resigned, persevering, and deeply reverent, for we must reflect that we are in the presence of a God and speaking with a Lord before Whom the Angels tremble out of respect and fear."
[St. Mary Magdalene de Pazzi 1566-1607]

Prayers and promises before the Beloved, along with the decoupling of ego power and the endless dying of the false self, the I-who-I-think-I-am, in order to serve the true Self – all these are tough calls. As Larry Dossey points out, we need to be careful with prayers and promises. What we offer may be called to account, what we ask for may be granted. And neither may be as we first thought or expected. Prayer to God matters, yes matters, for it is a spiritual co-creative process through which the world of matter can be transformed. Thus prayers and promises to God are serious stuff, arguably the most serious stuff. Perhaps St. Mary's "fear" language does not sit comfortably with the loving God we come to know, but to fear something in the spiritual sense is more concerned with notions of awe and respect rather than terror.

Oh, and the train dream? As a matter of interest it returned only once after ordination. The train went over and beyond the cliff. And just kept going.

Deep calls unto Deep

Jesus was a teacher of prayer. He is constantly praying, exhorting others to do likewise, going off alone or with others to pray. He not only taught us how to live, he taught us the means to do so – prayer. He was very clear about the kind of prayer too: not shouting aloud in public but, as the quote from Matthew's gospel at the beginning of this chapter indicates, going humbly into that private "inner space" to approach and be open to the presence and love of God. This is the work we do, this is our contribution, perhaps our only contribution, the only power we have – willingly setting self aside, making the effort for a while, if only a little while. The rest is up to the Divine. By paying attention and showing up, taking those first steps, we are saying "yes" to God. Setting aside those "no" moments enough for God to invade our lives, for the power of God's love to do its work in and through us, the only real power there is. We can only go so far with our own efforts. As I explored in *Coming Home* – DIY spirituality is a dubious route, and may even be harmful. Contemplatives, alone or in groups, are open to the guidance of others in turning their hearts to the God whose irresistible pull draws us to follow the Way.

It is common for some to want to give up, at any point, not just in the early stages. We can feel that we are "getting nowhere", that we have no time to pray or that ordinary life has encroached upon our prayer life so much that it has extinguished it. Yet these ego distractions are also part of the process – "patience, persistence and perseverance" are the watchwords (a useful meditation *mantra* in itself). And yet, though they may seem hopelessly infrequent, those "yes" moments are important, whether it be that brief moment of turning attention to God after months of distraction, or that one minute of longing for God in an hour of prayer that has been full of mental distractions and physical fidgets:

"It is a great mistake to believe that distractions are a sign that you can't pray, for what does it mean if you have a hundred and one distractions in say half an hour of prayer? It means that one hundred and one times you've turned away from distractions and turned back to God...that you have repeatedly said 'No' to self and 'Yes' to God, performed one hundred and one acts of selfless loving that have enabled you to die to the 'Old Man' so that the 'New Man' can be formed."
[David Torkington 1999 (The Prophet)]

David Torkington illuminates for us the inevitability of the experience of distraction and the essential hope in it. Quality not quantity is what matters in contemplation. The struggle is the sign that the inner transformative work of breaking down the old to release the new is under way. Without this dying and becoming, our consciousness stays stuck in a kind of living death (although the ego is convinced that without God it's quite happily alive thank you very much!):

"And so long as thou hast not that, this: Die and Become! Then thou art but a melancholy guest upon this dark earth."
[J W von Goethe 1749-1832]

The escape from the world of this "melancholy guest" is the contemplative Way - a way of the old self dying in order to become the fully realised Self. It is also paradoxically the way back into this world, but returning in a completely different place in ourselves. As we shall explore later, contemplation is not a permanent retreat from the world, but a stepping aside to be transformed and thus integrating both worlds to a point where there is no duality, just being in God in the world.

There are no magic formulas for contemplation. What works for one person may not work for another, what works at one time in our lives may not work at another. Nor do concepts like the "right way" or "being good or bad at it" have much meaning here. In contemplation there are no score cards, no points awarded for achieving spiritual highs, no goal posts where we can say we are "there", no certificates of expertise or professional qualifications. Sister Wendy's earlier quote on the simplicity of prayer is reinforced by Angela Ashwin on the practice of it:

"It doesn't matter how unsatisfactory or chaotic our lives are: prayer is still possible, because God is not waiting for us to become 'worthy' of a spiritual life, or experts in techniques. He simply asks us to open ourselves up to Him, so that he can be given space to love the bruised, muddled and selfish person we are. This is what prayer is about: God's love for us, and our response to that love - not our own so-called 'spiritual achievements'."
[Angela Ashwin 1990]

Contemplation is therefore less about technique and more about the consciousness, humility and intention with which we approach it. Thus it is not just for special people, but for those of good heart, who sincerely long for the love of God:

"The soul whose only desire is to be united to the Word of God and to be in fellowship with Him, will enter into the mysteries of His wisdom and knowledge as into the chambers of her heavenly Bridegroom."
[Origen c186-255]

Contemplatives are lovers of Love and are drawn to the Love that loves them like moths to a flame; drawn to the heavenly marriage of soul and God. A repeated leitmotif in the literature is the longing of the lover for the Beloved, the Bridegroom for the bride. Words like desire, hunger, longing, thirsting or weakness pepper the language of contemplatives. Words that in themselves, using language indicating deprivation or unquenchable desire, suggest the power of the soul's longing for its Beloved:

"My soul longs for Your Body; my heart desires to be united with You. Give me Yourself – it is enough; for without You there is no consolation. Without You I cannot exist, without your visitation I cannot live. I must often come to You, therefore, and receive the strength of my salvation, lest, deprived of this heavenly food, I grow weak on the way."
[Thomas à Kempis 1380-1471]

It is God who is seen as the source of true life, God's love that nourishes us so that we arise from a living death into that true life and see and participate in worldly life from that transformed view. Furthermore, the writers indicate that the thirsting never goes away; the contemplative always drinks from that deep well to sustain life. Any "methods" are there to support that shift of consciousness not ends in themselves, not so much the striving but the loving intention behind the striving is what matters:

"Strive first for the kingdom of God and his righteousness, and all these things will be given to you as well."
[Matthew 6:33]

Being single-minded, or perhaps more accurately being determinedly single-hearted in yearning for this Love, fuels the intention to draw ourselves closer to God, sets us on the Way. Some of that intensity of the fiery fuel is conveyed also by St. Francis:

"I beseech Thee, Oh Lord, that the fiery and sweet strength of Thy love may absorb my soul from all things that are under heaven, that I may die for love of Thy love as Thou didst deign to die for love of my love."
[St. Francis of Assisi c1181-1226]

This intensity seems to have an almost primordial quality to it, as if each soul has imprinted upon itself at the point of incarnation a destiny to reunite with its source:

"Creation is allowed in intimate love to speak to the Creator as if to a lover. As the Creator loves the creation, so the creation loves the Creator. The whole world has been embraced by this kiss."
[Hildegard of Bingen 1098-1179]

The magnetic pull between Creator and created is ultimately unassailable, but the mighty pull of "ordinary reality" to obstruct so many from breaking free seems overwhelming at times. However, the return Home, transcending concepts of space and time, is inevitable. No power is capable of ultimately getting in the way for the soul is its own intelligence, which is the same intelligence, the same knowledge of truth as the source from which it came. Love is drawn to love, truth to truth. The soul, like a hologram, is an imprint of the Divine; the part is inseperably the same as the whole:

"Each soul is a universe, 'unum versus alia omnia', because each soul is opened by reason of its intelligence to universal truth, and by its will to universal good. Each soul therefore is a spiritual universe which gravitates toward God, the sovereign good."
[Reginald Garrigou-Lagrange 1877-1964 (Life Everlasting)]

When Hadewijch, a thirteenth century mystic, sought to explain this power of the soul she resorted to ecstatic language. The soul is a way for God to be poured into the world, and it longs to be filled, each fulfilling the other. The soul, being incapable of possessing God in totality, is set in the dynamic of eternal longing, the desire of the lover for the Beloved:

"...now understand the deepest essence of your soul, what "soul" is. Soul is a being that can be held by God and by which, again, God can be beheld. Soul is also a being that wishes to contain God; it maintains a worthy state of being as long as it has not fallen beneath anything that is alien to it and less than the soul's own dignity. If it maintains this worthy state, the soul is a bottomless abyss in which God suffices to Himself; and His own self sufficiency ever finds fruition to the full in this soul, as a soul, for its part, ever does in Him. Soul is a way for the passage of God from his depths into his liberty; and God is a way for the passage of the soul into its liberty, that is, into its inmost depths, which cannot be touched except by the soul's abyss. And as long as God does not belong to the soul in its totality, He does not truly satisfy it."
[Hadewijch c13thC]

This soul longs to connect with its source and to manifest fully in the world, but it is as if the counter-magnetic pull of ordinary reality seduces it away from awareness of its source or at least traps it in a power source, the ego, from which it seems incapable of escape by its own devices. Sometimes a chink of weakness, a crack in the carapace, is the opening through which the power of the Divine breaks through. This fracturing of the ego's power can be in moments of realisation or wake up calls – perhaps through a "road to Damascus" intervention of the Divine, or maybe a sudden shattering of our view of the way we think things are, brought on by serious illness or falling in love or having a child; life events of many kinds that can shake us out of the status quo, cause us to question our current paradigm and open to a different view of reality. Such shifts of consciousness can awaken that primordial longing for reunion, for Home, for holy marriage:

> ***"I have no other dream than to conform myself at every moment with the suffering and Eucharistic life of our Divine Saviour, to unite my host with His Host, so that my heart may be consecrated with His Heart to the Glory of the Father for the salvation of the world. For the more my life is submitted to God and in conformity with the Redeemer, the more I shall participate in the achievement of His Work."***
> ***[Marthe Robin 1902-1981]***

Marthe Robin indicates that this awakening not only projects the soul into its return to God, but also awakens a willingness to be at work in the world, not for self-reward, but in service to others and for the Beloved. This reinforces the essential powerlessness of what we once thought of as powerful – our egos, our personalities, the identities in which we have invested who we think we are. Exposed, whether a little or stripped naked, the ego gives way and the soul comes into a recognition that it has no power of its own but the Source from which it springs:

> ***"I cannot dance O Lord, unless Thou lead me. If Thou wilt that I leap joyfully, then must Thou Thyself first dance and sing! Then will I leap for love, From love to knowledge, From knowledge to fruition, from fruition to beyond all human sense. There will I remain and circle evermore."***
> ***[Mechtilde of Magdeburg c1240-1298]***

To be open to that Source, the contemplative does not stop all activity in order to "switch off " (that would be to go to sleep or disconnect from the experience of reality), but sets aside all other experience and pays full attention to the awareness, to "see" and feel more deeply a Way towards the Source from which "all things visible and invisible" ultimately arise – God. The contemplative opens fully to both God and the world in unitive consciousness. That primordial drive, that awakening, that shift however great or small that projects us out of our established world view and opens us to the possibility of something "other" may be the starting point. It is the "faith": that sense of knowing that there is "more" even if we have not yet been able to define it or experience it deeply or have had our perceptions cluttered by the distortions or limitations of ideologies, theologies and philosophies. The hunger for Home is unleashed and is insatiable until it finds the source of nurturance, the Love of the Divine, on which it longs to feed and to which it longs to give itself.

Methods?

The inner prompting, however strongly or weakly felt, is the spark that ignites the search for the Way. This in turn opens us up to ways of deepening that search for that connection. For the contemplative the root is prayer. There is a map in this landscape, but it has few reference points. Our own methods can only take us so far. Much of the map is blank, where God leads us on that Way (although we can think for a while that it was ourselves who did all the work). Nevertheless we must follow the soul's promptings and try. Prayer is the closest to a "method" that the contemplative can be said to possess to help along this Way:

> ***"It is very simple. The most important task of any life that would respond fully to its potential is that we come into this light to be purified, to be made real, to discover our own divine potential. The term 'enlightenment' is used widely today, and for those of us who follow the footsteps of Christ, is an important term. We can only see with this light. What we see transforms who we are. We become, as St. John tells us, 'like him'."***
> ***[John Main 1926-82]***

John Main, one of the founders of the modern Christian meditation movement, encouraged a practice that drew upon the work of the desert fathers and mothers. A sacred word is used and repeated mantra-like to quieten the mind and draw the attention prayerfully towards God. The movement draws especially upon the Aramaic word *maranatha*, found in the writings of Paul [1 Cor. 16:22] and is translated as "Come, Lord", "Our Lord, Come" or "Our Lord has come". The first two interpretations are prayers seeking the return or presence of Christ, the last is more a declaration. It was used as a greeting between early Christians. John Main's work therefore taps into a very ancient tradition of mantric prayer in Christianity whether it be the use of sacred prayer words like *maranatha*, the Jesus Prayer (explored in detail later in this chapter) or the use of the rosary.

The practice has spread very widely and groups have sprung up across the world – demonstrating the heartfelt desire by so many to be still and silent in God. It is not universally acclaimed, as various very hostile websites demonstrate, but this seems not to have deterred its expansion. The hostility and intemperate language in some of the commentary offers some strange perspectives on what it is to be Christian! Certainly, some Christian denominations have difficulty with the concept of meditation and approaching God in this way. Others see it as leaning more towards contemplation than meditation. Words and phrases, usually from scripture, are important in contemplation too, but usually only as a source of prayerful focussing before opening to the Divine. While there is much debate about different methods and intentions in prayer, meditation and contemplation they draw from the same well, but just use the water differently and with some variation in intention, although always towards God.

For the contemplative, prayer is what helps along the Way. There are several universally tried and tested approaches that we can pursue confidently. Those who came before us, often centuries ago, have put themselves on the line and done the research for us. Many of them are cited in this book. As a general rule I recommend, "Use what works". Given the caveats expressed earlier about having proper guidance, there is a wide range of possibilities available to draw us ever more into those fruits of the spirit - the inner transformations and subsequent actions that come from the work of the Divine on the little self and soul:

> ***"Place your mind before the mirror of eternity! Place your soul in the brilliance of glory! And transform your entire being into the image of the Godhead Itself through contemplation."***
> ***[St. Clare of Assisi 1194-1253]***

A life of prayer is not a constant; we shift from day to day and mature in our approach to the Divine from childlike dependence on God as something separate from ourselves to union with the Divine in the spiritual marriage of the mystic. The myriad ways of being with God are all relevant and I do not suggest that any one is better or worse, each is but one of the infinite possibilities of entering into relationship with a God who is infinite. Growing in love with God is in some ways like growing in love with a person. I say this not to belittle the majesty of the Divine, but there are some parallels. In loving relationship with a person there are no limits to loving and discovery if we are willing to commit ourselves fully. The commitment to love someone means that we have to keep appointments, share meals, talk about experiences, be willing to be vulnerable, trusting, honest – the countless possibilities of connecting to and getting to know one another. In the same way there are no limits to relationship in the Beloved, the infinite of infinites, in whom love itself is not limited.

The contemplative is much less likely to feel lonely. Loneliness, as I explored in more detail in *Coming Home* and *Reflections on Spirituality and Health* has a direct impact upon health and wellbeing – it makes us sick. The contemplative is not lonely – how could we be when we are immersed in the All-that-is? Loneliness arises from separation, a consciousness of duality. The contemplative experiences non-duality, where 'God' and 'I' are not separate. It is the condition of being in Love, cultivated by requiring solitude at least occasionally that is a preferred separation and freedom from the distraction of others. Solitude is a choice, loneliness is unwanted disconnection. Solitude is needed when lover and Beloved can have time just to hang out together, time when 'together' loses its meaning in oneness in All-that-is.

This longing for being in Love is the root of the contemplative Way. We eschew interest in the spiritual materialism of a goal-oriented search for spiritual highs (which after all can be emulated with drugs) and, what goes with it, the avoidance of the lows when we come back down to earth. The contemplative lets go of such desires in favour of longing for a deepening of relationship with God. He or she is not in search of new acquisitions, but of deeper ways to surrender, to follow discipline, to fall into obedience so that the self is emptied of self to be possessed by Self:

> ***"Holy obedience binds our feet so that they no longer go their own way, but God's way. Children of the world say they are free when they are not subject to another's will, when no one stops them from satisfying their wishes and inclinations. For this dream of freedom, they engage in bloody battles and sacrifice life and limb. The children of God see freedom as something else. They want to be unhindered in following the Spirit of God; and they know that the greatest hindrances do not come from without, but lie within ourselves. Human reason and will, which would like so much to be their own masters, are unaware of their susceptibility to be swayed by natural inclinations and so to be enslaved by them. There is no better way of being freed of this slavery and receptive to the guidance of the Holy Spirit than that of holy obedience...In the poem of Goethe, most informed by the Christian spirit, he has his heroine say, 'Obedient, my soul felt free indeed.' "***
> ***[Sister Teresa Benedicta/Edith Stein 1891 -1942]***

Obedience in this sense (discussed in more detail in *Coming Home*) is not a kind of spiritual sado-masochism, but about disempowering the little self that has hitherto ruled our lives and held us back from the Self. It is about discerning what has heart and meaning for us in drawing us closer to God, in forgoing distractions that keep our attention away from the Divine. It is about turning off our own cacophony of inner voices to be still and listen deeply (the roots of the word 'obedience' lie in 'listening' or 'lending an ear'). In doing so, we also have to consider the inner work on our interior distractions, unhealed wounds, neuroses and desires for power, control or acclaim – the 'sins' such as pride and avarice, things which distract us from our true purpose. In the practice of virtue, itself a spiritual practice, we help to break the power of the ego. It can be as simple as preferring to pray rather than party, to pay attention to God through *lectio divina* rather than watch TV, to be silent rather than argue, to do voluntary work rather than engage in promiscuity, to engage lovingly with a partner, family and friends rather than stay longer at work. That is not to say that partying or watching TV is wrong and must be abandoned, rather it is to set such things in context and in proportion in our lives. It is about surrender; emptying out of some things to make space and time for God:

"Now seeing virtues dispose us to contemplation, it behoveth us to use the means that may bring us to virtues. And they be three means which men most commonly use that give themselves to contemplation: as reading of holy scripture and good books, secondly, spiritual meditation; thirdly, diligent prayer with devotion…thus: Blessed are the clean in heart, for they shall see God. In meditation, likewise, shalt thou see those virtues which be needful for thee to have, as humility, mildness, patience, righteousness, spiritual strength, temperance, cleanness, peace and soberness, faith, hope and charity. These virtues thou shalt see in meditation, how good, how fair, how profitable they be; and by prayer thou shalt thereupon desire and get them."
[Walter Hilton c1340-1396]

Spiritual practices, as opportunities for obedience or 'listening in' to our higher calling, are presented to us at every moment. Coming to know every aspect of our being is part of the work of the contemplative. It is not possible to sit in bliss and be of service in the world unless the emotional work has also been undertaken. Otherwise, whatever enlightenments we receive risk being corrupted by our neuroses and other egoic influences:

"We can never know God until we first know clearly our own soul."
[Mother Julian of Norwich c1342-1416]

The commitment to know ourselves so that we may be free to know God demands obedience to follow that journey. For, as we discussed earlier, knowing and healing ourselves is not always a pain-free process so the serious spiritual seeker sets in place the support that is needed along the Way – the Soul Friends and so forth. While we can play our part in working and seeking support for that work, it is worth remembering that the contemplative is not alone. People are supportive, but we draw upon the Beloved and intentionally so. Thus the literature from contemplatives is littered with prayers expressing the realisation of the limitations of our own resources; full of pleas seeking God's assistance, such as that embodied in these words:

> ***"O my God, Trinity whom I adore; help me to forget myself entirely that I may be established in You as still and as peaceful as if my soul were already in eternity. May nothing trouble my peace or make me leave You, O my Unchanging One, but may each minute carry me further into the depths of Your mystery. Give peace to my soul; make it Your heaven, Your beloved dwelling and Your resting place. May I never leave You there alone but be wholly present, my faith wholly vigilant, wholly adoring, and wholly surrendered to Your creative Action...O Eternal Word, Word of my God, I want to spend my life in listening to You, to become wholly teachable that I may learn all from You. Then, through all nights, all voids, all helplessness, I want to gaze on You always and remain in Your great light. O my beloved Star, so fascinate me that I may not withdraw from Your radiance...O consuming Fire, Spirit of Love, "come upon me," and create in my soul a kind of incarnation of the Word...O my Three, my All, my Beatitude, infinite Solitude, Immensity in which I lose myself, I surrender myself to You as Your prey. Bury Yourself in me that I may bury myself in You until I depart to contemplate in Your light the abyss of Your greatness."***
>
> ***[Elizabeth of the Trinity 1880-1906]***

Notice the language of love in this prayer, the expressions of longing, the willingness to surrender, the pleading for help to do so, the all-consuming nature of the fire of that love (a subject to which we will turn shortly). No part of us escapes the "all-consuming fire"; we need to be taken care of as we plunge deeper into those flames and to be properly prepared for the process.

The preparation takes different forms in different traditions. Periods of fasting, isolation, *lectio divina*, being subject to the guidance of a director – these are the grist to the mill in some contemplative schools. Common to all, however, is the requirement to deepen the practice of prayer. A few general principles can be drawn out at this point, with the caveat that this is not a rigid formula, but options for guidance:

1. Commitment - making a conscious intention to daily prayer, as frequently as this is feasible. Personally I set aside time each day, usually 9am and 9pm, not least because a community to which I belong, the Iona Community, is often also in prayer at these times. I have been on retreats with different faiths where prayer time is set aside 5, 7, 12 or more times per day, sometimes for half an hour or more at a time, sometimes for just a few moments. This commitment is about cultivating a turning of our awareness towards God, making time for God and sticking with it, until it becomes second nature; perhaps moving us to a point where there is no contemplative time and non-contemplative time. Our lives become contemplation:

"We must know before we can love. In order to know God we must often think of Him; and when we come to love Him, we shall then also think of Him often, for our heart will be with our treasure....By the practice of the presence of God, by steadfast gaze on Him, the soul comes to a knowledge of God, full and deep, to an unclouded vision. All its life is passed in unceasing acts of love and worship, of contrition and of simple trust, of praise and prayer, and service. At times indeed life seems to be but one long unbroken practice of His divine presence."
[Brother Lawrence 1614-1691]

2. Preparation – getting physically comfortable, making sure we can have uninterrupted quietness and so on, as discussed earlier. In this we ready ourselves, shifting our attention from our time to God time. This might include lectio divina or other words to inspire us, meditation or a general opening prayer:

"The soul...to penetrate revealed truths...meditates upon them, making use of a book if necessary; it brings them together and draws practical consequences which leads it to turn more and more fully toward God. This is the human work of understanding, which rather rapidly becomes simplified, like reading in the case of a child who no longer needs to spell. Meditation thus becomes a very simple, affective prayer, an active recollection which is a preparation or disposition to receive the grace of contemplation."
[Reginald Garrigou-Lagrange 1877-1964 (Christian Perfection and Contemplation)]

3. Greeting God – acknowledging God's presence

4. Talking to God – getting stuff off our chest, things that we want to say sorry for, things that bother us.

5. Appreciating God - for being there, offering thanks for all the blessings in life.

6. Asking of God – if there are things we want of God; there's no need to beat about the bush or fritter our attention away on why we should bother asking if God knows everything anyway or whether God is there or not. Ask anyway. Remember (see Coming Home) that prayer is not just about thinking about or talking to God, it is a way we relate to God. Even though we do not experience God as separate or if we know that God knows what we want before we ask anyway, an interior dialogue can still happen. After all, just because we can talk to people who know us very well and can tell us what we think before we think it, we don't stop talking to them. The talking is one way we form a relationship with a person. No less so than with God. Getting all theoretical and questioning about prayer, whether we are doing it the right way or the wrong way, whether prayer "works" or not – these are just distractions. We can use prayers known to us such as the Lord's Prayer or make one up. It is fine to pray as we can, not as we can't:

> ***"Each prayer is more beautiful than the others. I cannot recite them all and not knowing which to choose, I do like children who do not know how to read, I say very simply to God what I wish to say, without composing beautiful sentence, and He always understands me. For me, prayer is an aspiration of the heart, it is a simple glance directed to heaven, it is something great, supernatural, which expands my soul and unites me to Jesus."***
> ***[Therese of Lisieux 1873-1897]***

7. Shutting up – the talking gives way to being silent before God so that we might hear what God wants us to hear.

8. Promising to act – on what we feel God is guiding us to do (but see the cautions above about checking this for veracity later as discussed earlier, and in detail in *Coming Home*)

9. Deepening the silence – the mind can run riot with things to think about. Prayer is full of potential distraction. The Buddhists call this "monkey mind". Like a monkey swinging through the treetops grabbing one branch after another, so the mind snatches at thoughts one after another. There's no point in getting into battle with our minds here, indeed that's one of the tricks of the power-hungry ego to keep us distracted. Our "prayer of the heart" (explored in more detail later) gives the mind something with which to occupy itself and sets us free to deepen the stillness:

"What's important to remember is that these phrases are not only used to keep helping you turn back to God from the distractions that would turn you away from Him. Don't try to dwell on them. They're not to help you meditate, but to contemplate"
[David Torkington 1995 (The Mystic)]

We might use our breathing to help us pay attention, to quieten the mind and open us more to the Presence, by aligning it with our prayer. A word or phrase can help us turn back to God when we get distracted or to pierce the cloud that keeps us from God. As prayer deepens we see the distractions but are not governed by them. The repetition of our sacred prayer words readies us to be open to the Presence:

"Pray not in many words but in a little word of one syllable. Fix this word fast to your heart so that it is always there come what may. With this word you will suppress all thoughts."
[Anon. 14thC (The Cloud of Unknowing)]

10. Let God be God - our prayer, having launched us out of ourselves, opens us and makes us more receptive to God's loving presence. We let go of our expectations, words, thoughts and other attachments. Just sitting, we wait, available to the One who reaches out to us in love:

"God wants souls to achieve this end without the intervention of actions by setting them at once in contemplation. So what previously the soul was gaining gradually through its labour of meditation on particular facts has now through practice changed into a habit of loving knowledge, of a general kind, and not distinct as before. Therefore when the soul gives itself to prayer it is now like one to whom water has been brought, so that he drinks peacefully, without labour, and is no longer forced to draw the water through the aqueducts of past meditations and forms and figures. Then, as soon as the soul comes before God, it makes an act of knowledge, loving, passive and tranquil, in which it drinks of wisdom and love and delight"
[St. John of the Cross 1542-1591 (The Ascent of Mount Carmel)]

Here, in this "condition of complete simplicity" (Eliot) we put down our efforts to acquire, define, possess and all the other attempts of the mind to fix things. Words, images and other prompts are no longer needed, but they are available to us to return to should we be pulled away for any reason. Being in God, receptive to the love and the gaze of God, the soul returns that loving gaze; one love, one gaze:

"When you are praying, do not shape within yourself any image of the Deity, and do not let your intellect be stamped with the impress of any form; but approach the Immaterial in an immaterial manner, and then you will understand."
[St. Isaiah the Solitary c420-491]

Thus, ten points for guidance towards the contemplative Way, but guidance is all they are. Please use 'what works', but as always test it with your Soul Friend. Different forms or aspects of prayer can be used at different times. Some prefer that all prayer begins with gratitude and so always prepare this way. Others, after a while, may find that a lot of preparation is unnecessary and can begin by going directly to our "prayers of the heart" in which all the various 'steps' are implicit. Indeed, we may notice that words like 'begin' and 'end' start to mean very little here. We may come to see the blessings of 'sometimes less is more' as we find a sacred word or phrase becomes a prayer on our lips and in our hearts all the time. Simplicity in prayer towards contemplation is often a sign of maturation along the Way. In part this simplicity leads us to a place of confidence that our prayer-longing for connection to God will indeed be heard. If we do not yet trust at this level then that is an indicator of more of the emotional work to be done accompanied by our Soul Friend or perhaps counsellor or therapist:

"Therefore, reciting even now the same words, let each person be confident, for God will pay heed quickly to those who make supplications through these."
[Athanasius 295-373]

Down the years I have become acquainted with prayers from many traditions, but I find that nowadays I have settled into just a few. They come and go in my life, being ladders of ascent or descent and towers of strength at the appropriate time. I have included some of these in the prayer suggestions at the end of this book.

Although the above steps begin with a willingness to commit, there is paradox here too. We cannot come fully into contemplation if we are attached to it. The desire to achieve some kind of goal, fulfilment, enlightenment or union with God – all these get in the way. It is the longing of the heart that propels us, not the demands of the ego and sometimes it can be hard to distinguish between the two. Our 'false selves' or egos tell us we are subjects ripe for special and unique experiences. Contemplatives embrace their fundamental ordinariness. The ego puffs up with ambition, a sense of entitlement and a hunger for the next experience; it seeks the highs and avoids the lows. The longing of the heart knows only humility and with that the willingness to surrender; waiting upon God. The ego is impatient, gives up easily, tells us all kinds of reasons why we should give up; the heart will wait forever although it knows it will not have to.

Contemplation is showing up before and in God, surrendering to a relationship with God in which God takes us where God wills. It requires trust, an inner relationship to or hope of the Divine, a presumption of faith that God is real. Some great contemplatives have argued that faith, however unformed, must precede contemplation. It requires us to find a degree of trust in that loving God, to know that whatever happens as we approach God we will be safe and taken care of. Others are full of doubt about faith. Perhaps the answer is to simply pray anyway, and wait in the contemplative Way.

Saints and scholars down the ages have argued whether contemplation is a special gift of God for a privileged and blessed few or an inherent quality of all people, whether faith must precede an experience of God or whether an experience can produce faith. The arguments make for interesting theological debates. To be contemplative is possible for all human beings simply because it is the quality in-and-of everyone, however inhibited, damaged or distracted by upbringing or lifestyle. We are all ensouled. It may sometimes seem that the potential is buried deep, but there is that of God in everyone, as the Quaker faith holds, and this truth makes possible the contemplative Way for all. It is not a requirement, there may be other ways to God, but our humanity embodies the capacity for contemplation; the receptacle for the gift of the Divine. The effort, our effort, is to put ourselves into the condition in which this nature can act: a *kenosis* (self emptying) as Thomas Merton illuminates:

> ***"An emptiness that is deliberately cultivated, for the sake of fulfilling personal spiritual ambition, is not empty at all: it is full of itself. It is so full that the light of God cannot get into it anywhere; there is not a crack or a corner left where anything else can wedge itself into this hard core of self-aspiration...In the contemplative life, it is neither desire nor the refusal of desire that counts, but only that 'desire' which is a form of 'emptiness,' that is to say which acquiesces in the unknown and peacefully advances where it does not see the way. All the paradoxes about the contemplative way are reduced to this one: being without desire means being led by a desire so great that it is incomprehensible."***
> ***[Thomas Merton 1915-1968 (Contemplative Prayer)]***

The contemplative freely chooses God and in so doing comes to see the traps of the desire, which can fill us. When filled with our wishes for reaching goals of higher states of consciousness, nirvana, enlightenment or bliss – these inhibit us. Furthermore, one of the tricks of the ego, when it realises it cannot control the soul, is a tendency to possess everything, including our spiritual life. It is as if it says, "Oh, I can't win this one" or "This looks like fun"... "So I'll take charge of it."! A good Soul Friend is needed to help us empty ourselves of blockages like this.

The desire for the experience of God is full of paradox, fuelling the urge towards God yet carrying with it the need to be surrendered in order to approach God. It is the "desireless desire" , which is replaced by – what? Hope and waiting. The kind of hope rooted in faith. The kind of waiting where expectation is renounced, all desire is suspended and we get ourselves out of the way. Waiting not as in a queue but as in quiet expectation for as little or as long as it takes.

Contemplatives cultivate *kenosis* to open the space in which God can be at work in us and through us in the world. There is no space if every moment of our lives is crowded with the busyness of activity whether physical or mental. We live in a world where the senses can be flooded with stimulation from relentless demands and distractions – background television, endless 24 hour communication by telephone or text or email, long hours of work, family and other commitments. If we find time for an interior life we can get just as busy with that too, filling the inner space with spiritual materialism – the desires for experience, of getting enlightened, of achieving some spiritual goal. All these can crowd out our awareness of the Presence. All must be renounced if we are to be receptive to the spirit of the Beloved, to be occupied not by our own preoccupations but by God. Then, perhaps with discipline and diligence, we may reach a point where all aspects of our lives have been colonised by God. If the spiritual life has any goal at all then it is this: simply to let God's love invade our lives completely.

Engaged with the World

Through this invasion of the love of the Beloved our lives are transformed – "saved". We look out upon and act in the world from a different vantage point. Through annihilation of the power of the false self in the Divine the space we once filled is full-filled by God. However, thus filled the contemplative does not abandon the world :

> ***"There are some who foolishly imagine perfection to consist in this, that they being quiet and free, can dismiss images from the intellect, and with mere idle sensuality can retire into themselves; neglecting meanwhile the love of God, and all pious works and exercises...following after false quiet...Legitimate cultivators of contemplation and supernatural quiet, so seek after a denuded mind...yet they do not abandon good works and exercises."***
> ***[Louis of Blois 1506-1566]***

We do not disconnect completely from daily concerns or lapse into quietism, abandoning the world to its fate from a place of passive retreat and assume that God will sort it all out. Rather, the contemplative becomes more engaged, more connected to the world, feels its joys and its sufferings more and willingly embraces them all. This stems from a completely different perspective than of old - no longer gripped by the need for ego gratification or the desire to avoid suffering, no longer enthralled by the desire for power to change the world and cast it in our own image or the power to escape it. We die into life; dead to the power of the little self and born into the power of the soul. There arises instead a willingness to surrender completely into service as opposed to being self-serving:

> ***"Pray as though everything depended on God. Work as though everything depended on you."***
> ***[St. Augustine 354-430]***

Until we encounter God we act from the perspective of the ego, of the personal, with all the potential to do good in the world – and to do harm. Surrender into and experience of Divine love allows us to let go of our ego agendas and to work from the transpersonal, to love and work in service to the Will when our own will has been wrestled into submission and service. In being reduced, we are magnified, in being emptied, we are made full, in being broken we are made whole. A different kind of happiness arises that is not contingent upon attachment to transient, worldly things:

"Hence it is we see what the highest aim of our theology is, that from it we may learn the way to the Supreme Good, and may make this life to become a ladder by which we may advance step by step to the eternal happiness awaiting us."
[Peter of Alcantara 1499-1562]

Happiness that is self-seeking is not eternal. Captured by the love of God, our own happiness is not complete without engaging with the world to nurture the happiness of others. As we plunge deeper into God and God plunges deeper into our lives, we find ourselves strengthened to live authentically. We come to 'walk our talk' – willing to be more caring of each other, the environment and ourselves and to live virtuously and in harmony with our values:

No law or commandment can prevent a person from desecrating the holiness that is life, or force a person to not harm. Only the heart understands nonharm, nonviolence. Only the heart has the wisdom to realise the sanctity of life. Only compassion, the truth of our sensitivity can change humanity.
[Beverly Lanzetta 2015]

The "battle" to overcome duality, of separation between ordinary reality and the transcendent, of the material and the numinous, is resolved simply because we learn to accept differentiation, a deep awareness that we are held in God and individual at the same time. In this surrender we do nothing, we are not exhausted or burned out by the need to care, succeed, achieve or make things happen – rather the caring and succeeding happen through us. We no longer have to 'do' compassion with effort; rather it is the effortless effort of letting compassion, *the* compassion, suffuse our being and become available in us for others. We do not work less in the world, indeed we may work more but we do not own the work, rather we work "for the honour of the one" out of whom we came [John 7:17]:

"But to love one's neighbour with perfect justice it is necessary to be prompted by God. How can you love your neighbour with purity if you do not love him in God? But he who does not love God cannot love in God. You must first love God, so that in Him you can love your neighbour too."
[Bernard of Clairvaux 1090-1153]

Loving one's neighbour in God, in whatever form of service that takes, is a world away from many aspects of service where we do all the work from our own inner resources. Our false self batteries are finite and all our actions, social, political or personal, risk being corrupted by the destructive and finite influence of ego power. Love of and surrender to the Divine Will negates the possibility of an ego takeover. Working in the world from this connection to God draws on a boundless source. There is no exhaustion or burnout here. We act as servants in the world, the power of the Divine working in and through us cannot be burned out.

The Fire and Water of Holy Love

"And immediately the eyes of my soul were opened and I beheld the plenitude of God, whereby I did comprehend the whole world, both here and beyond the sea, and the abyss and all things else; and therein did I behold naught save the divine power in a manner assuredly indescribable, so that through excess of marvelling the soul cried with a loud voice, saying, 'The whole world is full of God!' "
[Angela of Foligno 1248-1309]

Count Almasy in Michael Ondaatje's *The English Patient* says, "The heart is an organ of fire". The heart we consider here, in the life of the contemplative, is not merely the physical heart, or the heart as a metaphor for the emotions or the seat of erotic love. Rather it is the heart as described in some of the earliest contemplative literature, the seat of the soul, the very essence of our being, the source of love of all (*agape*) unbounded by ego desires (see, for example, the exploration of different understandings of love in *Coming Home*).

Spiritual practices such as prayer and the study of the Divine (for example theology or reading about spirit) can only take us so far. We can learn about the love of God from a good book or an inspirational teaching. We can get a taste from these of what it might be. Contemplatives seek that love which can only be known by experience, by feeling and knowing it deeply. Personal effort such as daily prayer is important and unavoidable; it prepares the way. The effort is important, but it is a gentle trying, being ready to set it down and to be open. The contemplative commits to creating the space to open to this love and to let it to burst through into every aspect of our being and daily life. We become transformed in the way we are and what we do. This transformation is experienced as a powerful inner shift of consciousness, so powerful that words to describe it across the spectrum of contemplative writers draw upon metaphors of fire and water. Richard Rolle expresses this theme in his fourteenth century treatise called *The Fire of Love*:

"I have wondered more than I can tell, when first I felt my heart grow warm, and glow with no imaginary, but with a real, and as it were, sensible flame. So I marvelled when that flame first burst forth in my soul, and was in unwonted peace, through the unexpectedness of this abundance.... For I had not reckoned that such a warmth could happen to any man in this exile, ... for even as a finger, placed in the fire, is clothed with heat which it feels, so the soul, kindled in this manner, as I have told, is sensible of the most real heat; but now fiercer and greater, now less, even as the frailty of the flesh allows. Therefore I offer this book to the sight - not of philosophers and wise men of the world, nor of great theologians wrapped in endless questionings, but of the simple and untaught, those who seek to love God rather than to know many things. For not by disputing, but by doing is He known, and by loving. Wherefore, because here I incite all to love, and I shall seek to explain the burning and supernatural feeling of love, let this book be allotted the title of Fire of Love."
[Richard Rolle 1290-1349]

Once we encounter this fire, there is no going back. Day by day, year by year, the accretions of the ego are singed away, its power reduced to ashes sometimes blissfully, sometimes painfully. Under the relentless attention of this holy fire of love, the ego's (or what some would call the "diabolic or demonic force", see *Coming Home*) role as master of our lives is broken; it shifts to being the servant of our lives in God. If we fall into forgetting from time to time, contemplation calls us into remembrance.

There can be many times in this process that ordinary life can seem unbearable, the company of others and the ordinary sights and sounds of life excruciating. The fire affects our perception of the world and sensitises us to things which are false to fact or un-nurturing :

"The man who has known the odour of heavenly fire runs from a gathering of men, like a bee from smoke, since smoke drives off a bee just as company militates against a man."
[John Climacus c525-606]

But it is not the destiny of most of us to run permanently from the company of others, although there can be periods when retreat is necessary perhaps over many days and weeks. Every contemplative I have ever encountered has integrated some retreat time not just away from home and work but also into our daily lives, in the sense of ensuring time each day of stillness, silence and solitude. I met Eileen Caddy some years ago. She was one of the inspirational founders of the Findhorn community in Scotland, which was to become a major influence in the expression of modern spirituality. She told me that while trying to raise a family in a cramped caravan the only place of solitude she could find each day was to go to the camp-site toilets and lock herself in a cubicle to meditate! Fortunately most of us can find more comfortable locations, at least at some point in the day! But then the place in some respects does not matter, for there is nowhere that God is not. By finding a place outside and inside ourselves to be still, the "still small voice" can be heard:

"When both thy intellect and will are quiet and passive to the expressions of the eternal Word and Spirit, and when thy soul is winged up above that which is temporal, the outward senses and the imagination being locked up by holy abstraction, then the eternal Hearing, Seeing and Speaking will be revealed in thee. Blessed art thou therefore if thou canst stand still from self thinking and self willing, and canst stop the wheel of thy imagination and senses."
[Jakob Boehme 1575-1624]

Quelling the senses and their attention upon the exterior world, the inner world explodes with all its truth and beauty. Hearing, seeing, feeling, smelling, touching continue but at a profoundly different level. The self is purged. Illumination bursts into the available space. Awareness expands:

"The soul, leaving all things and forgetting herself, is immersed in the ocean of Divine Splendour, and illuminated by the Sublime Abyss of the Unfathomable Wisdom."
[Dionysius (Pseudo-Dionysius) the Areopagite c6thC]

From Dionysius we receive the oceanic metaphor of this illumination, seeking to convey its enormity and majesty. Yet this grandeur is also minute, for it is being witnessed within us. I enjoy watching a popular UK television series called *Dr. Who*. This fantasy programme has the character of the time-travelling doctor shift around the universe in a rather miniscule and ordinary-looking police telephone box. Actually, not many of these blue icons are seen in UK towns and cities these days, although they were a common sight in my childhood. The Doctor's mode of travel is really a time machine called the *Tardis* in disguise. However, step through the doors and an enormous space reveals itself. Contemplation is like that, an encounter with impossible astonishing spaciousness contained within our own tiny consciousness.

Maritime metaphors are again taken up and mixed with fire to describe the experience by St. Catherine of Siena:

> ***"O unfathomable depth! O Deity eternal! O deep ocean! What more could You give me than to give me Yourself? You are an ever-burning Fire; You consume and are not consumed. By Your fire, You consume every trace of self-love in the soul. You are a Fire, which drives away all coldness and illumines minds with its light, and with this light You have made known Your truth. Truly this light is a sea which feeds the soul until it is all immersed in You, O peaceful Sea, eternal Trinity! The water of this sea is never turbid; it never causes fear, but gives knowledge of the truth. This water is transparent and discloses hidden things; and a living faith gives such abundance of light that the soul almost attains to certitude in what it believes."***
> ***[St. Catherine of Siena 1347-1380]***

Light, fire, flooding are also sprinkled in the language of the modern day Roman Catholic mystic and scientist Teilhard de Chardin. He discovers in his experience that his longing was not to possess God but to be possessed. In so doing he comes to see that this fire of love is the very engine of the creation, invisibly holding and penetrating every atom and the entire fabric of the universe:

"When your presence, Lord, has flooded me with its light I hoped that within it I might find ultimate reality at its most tangible. But now that I have in fact laid hold on you, you who are utter consistency, and feel myself borne by you, I realise that my deepest hidden desire was not to possess you but to be possessed. It is not as radiation of light nor as subtilised matter that I desire you; nor was it thus that I described you in my first intuitive encounter with you: it was as fire. And I can see I shall have no rest unless an active influence, coming forth from you, bears down on me to transform me. The whole universe is aflame."
[Teilhard de Chardin 1881-1955 (The Hymn of the Universe)]

In this famous phrase "the whole universe is aflame" he seeks to describe the radiant power of the Divine. There is nowhere and no-thing that is not of and in God, carrying in its very nature the Divine fire. The mystic's vision goes beyond ordinary comprehension of reality, of the limitations of the five senses operating in material reality. We "see", "feel" and "know" in ways that words cannot fully capture. The inner fire of love of and from God is the transforming power at work, beyond our full comprehension, nevertheless felt and experienced personally and intimately. It changes us inwardly, doing its work until we are stilled and readied:

"When the fire acts, igniting the wood and setting it ablaze, then the fire reduces the wood to something small, quite unlike its former self, removing from it its bulk, coldness, mass and moistness, and making the wood more and more like itself. And yet neither the fire, nor the wood is satisfied or contented with any warmth, heat or likeness until fire has given birth to itself in the wood and has conveyed to it its own nature and its own being so that all becomes single fire, equally one, without distinction and knowing neither increase nor decrease. And that is why, until the process is complete, there is always smoke, crackling and contention between the fire and the wood. But when all the differences between them have been removed, the fire is still and the wood is silent."
[Meister Eckhart c1260-1328]

The fire being still and the wood silent, the contemplative is not left sitting in bliss and disconnected from the world, rather he or she is engaged with it, knowing the whole universe is aflame, becoming a willing participant in the healing of the brokenness of human consciousness and conduct in ways large or small.

Our contemplative surrender offers us a constant preparation to be open to God's love. Like some people take a run or do aerobics, contemplative prayer is our daily spiritual exercise, the exercise of the human heart. It draws us out of ourselves and into God. Even if we feel our prayer life is sloppy and weak, the fact that we make that commitment of time and effort allows us, however ineptly, to have moments, increasing numbers of moments, when we are being less self-absorbed and more self-less in God. In time, perhaps a lifetime, we find that surrender into the Divine is experienced more and more so that we have fewer and fewer episodes of falling into forgetting, into old ego-driven patterns, and more and more time "in the temple"; at one in God. Being in the world of deep connection to the Beloved is what all the spiritual teachers down the ages from all backgrounds have taught us – this is the "fruit of the spirit":

"But the fruit of the spirit is love, joy, peace, longsuffering, kindness, goodness, faithfulness, gentleness, self-control."
[Galatians 5:22]

The expression of these fruits of the spirit, however, does not come from that laborious place of trying to be moral, to do good. It comes as we explored earlier from a deep and authentic relaxation into the Divine love working through us. Thus we are not doing good, rather letting the good emerge through us from its inexhaustible source; the way of action without burnout. The transforming fire of the contemplative Way sets us free of this labour. By coming to love God and be loved by God, we are liberated into serving from the heart. This serving of love rather than trying to do love is the "effortless effort".

As the contemplative Way awakens us, we find a renewed commitment to the world. Yet it does not mean that we all have to go off and set up a feeding station for the hungry in a far away country or some high profile grand scheme to heal the world's sick or relieve universal poverty. This God of love is the God of small things, what we do in our local community unsung or unseen is a manifestation of this love too. It starts right under our noses:

> ***"...the contemplative way of prayer and life also includes a strong commitment to a local congregation, commitment to its worship and prayer, fellowship and care, witness and mission. I realise that this thought may be uncomfortable for some, but this nevertheless is true. You should be able to take your experience of silence into the life of your church."***
> ***[Peter Dodson and MartinTunnicliffe 2005]***

Love is not measured by quantity but by quality. What we do for and with one we do for all. One act of love in our own homes is as powerful an action we might take on what we think is a grander scale. The contemplative Way expands our capacity to be more loving, more present, more engaged where we are right now:

> ***"When the soul is naughted and transformed, then of herself she neither works nor speaks nor wills, nor feels nor hears nor understands; neither has she of herself the feeling of outward or inward, where she may move. And in all things it is God who rules and guides her, without the meditation of any creature....And she is so full of peace that though she pressed her flesh, her nerves, her bones, no other thing come forth from them than peace."***
> ***[Catherine of Genoa 1447-1510]***

Thus we come to live for ourselves more fully and more for others, experiencing the oneness of the creation, the "being-bliss-awareness" (*sat-cit-ananda* - the unchanging reality known in the Hindu tradition as Brahman) through being reborn into the world, seeing truth and all things new. This is the dying into life to which Jesus calls us – out of the dead zone of limited perceptions of self and material reality and into living life from the transcendent all-embracing divine vision. We are born again into a new life having lived a life where the "dead bury the dead" [Luke 9:60]. For life lived before this transformation, in which so many live without knowing otherwise, seems like a death. Our experience of ordinary existence without the sense of being full-filled deep within can seem empty and ultimately fruitless. We seek to fill this emptiness with a thousand addictions from sex to shopping, TV to travel. The contemplative is God filled. He or she still en-joys the world; encounters the suffering in it, but responds to it differently. Being filled with love enables us to be comforted no matter the situation in which we find ourselves. Love makes us spiritually resilient, tough:

"All consolation that does not come from God is but desolation; when the soul has learned to receive no comfort but in God only, it has passed beyond the reach of desolation.'
[Madame Guyon 1648-1717]

Even "desolations" are responded to differently. Being infused by love, see-ing the "universe aflame", knowing deeply (in the words of Mother Julian) that "All shall be well" – all these liberate us to embrace suffering, including our own, with greater equanimity:

"The man who has known pure joy, if only for a moment...is the only man for whom affliction is something devastating. At the same time he is the only man who has not deserved the punishment. But, after all, for him it is no punishment; it is God holding his hand and press-ing rather hard. For, if he remains constant, what he will discover buried deep under the sound of his own lamentations is the pearl of the silence of God."
[Simone Weil 1909-1943]

Many different faiths, not least Christianity, rest on the knowledge that there is no separation between ourselves and God. That separation or duality is an illusion (brought on by egoic distortions, woundedness, the distractions of material reality, the work of demonic forces - depending on your point of view). The scene at the time of the crucifixion, where the temple curtain is torn apart, is profoundly symbolic of the truth of non-du-ality. A recent visit to Iona reinforced this for me.

For over 30 years this island has drawn me. Now, having crossed many times that stretch of water from Mull (only a mile, but always it seems I leave the world behind) as visitor, tourist and pilgrim, I return often as teacher and guide. I help to organise retreats for those who want to "come home" and this special place, where it is said the veil between this world and the next is thinnest, seems especially gifted in nourishing the soul. While I have to "work" there, I also make sure that I set aside time between sessions for quietness and reflection, to take long walks in the low hills and along the magnificent beaches. Iona is such an elemental place – extremes of weather and landscape, the encircling sea – helping you to strip away perceptions of ordinary life and sink more deeply into a sense of the sacred.

One day I went to the abbey as usual in the early hours for some time of solitary prayer. It never closes, nor do most of the other churches and prayer rooms on the island - a precious gift, for in other settings these days such sacred places are often locked when not in use. I went down to the altar. Someone had left the Bible resting on that glorious great slab of white marble veined with serpentine. It happened to be open at the story of the crucifixion and my eyes were drawn to the passage about the curtain of the temple being torn apart at the point when Jesus dies [Mark 15:38]. And here I was, in the temple, with no curtain separating me from the altar. The abbey church is one of the few Christian places I visit regularly where there is no rail or barrier between people and altar. It is open, inviting, welcoming. It is as if the tearing of the veil at the time of Jesus' death was a reminder that his service, among other things, was to tear down the veil that separates people from God. Jesus opened the uncluttered Way to the Divine. Hitherto, the centre of the Jerusalem temple had been shrouded by linen curtains and only the high priest could enter this "holy of holies", the place of the Presence. Jesus proletarianised God, removing any separation from God and the people of God.

I sat down for a while and became very aware that not only is there no physical separation between altar and people, but also and that it is not a place of grand, even intimidating, ascent. In so many holy places the high altar, the holy of holies, is just that – high – and placed at some level above the congregation. It is common practice to go up steps into a church then ascend more steps to the altar. Stepping up to something is loaded with symbols and values, but I was struck by how in the abbey church as in only one other church I know (Worth Abbey) we descend to the altar. The main entrance of the abbey is on higher ground than the building's focus of worship. Like the absence of a barrier, this too seems meaningful. A gentle slope downhill seems to embody so much less effort. It is as if the altar on Iona beckons with an easy aspect of faith, that it does not always have to be hard work, that we do not always have to climb, that God is below us as well as above us - supporting, accessible, receptive, within reach.

This accessibility opens us to the consciousness of the eternal (not the same as forever – eternity is not governed by time and space). The mystery of the resurrection invites us in. To the contemplative, this is more than debates about the theology of bodily resurrection. Christ is set free of space and time; thus freed is always and readily available to our consciousness. Jesus while embodied was available to only the few who would meet him. Liberated from the body the cosmic Christ consciousness is, always has been, always will be, available in the eternal now, everywhere and anywhere.

In the abbey church of Iona and the Iona Community we encounter not only the mystic Christ, but also find this God grounded in the inclusive - in the liturgy and song of the Community, the programmes that reach out to seekers everywhere, its action for social justice, its family groups around the world, the essence of service that emanates from every one who works in it. This open-armed Beloved is found in the buildings and the people who invite and welcome. Little wonder then that so many people who come to this island and this sacred space of worship find their faith and relationship in the One challenged, renewed, refreshed or, in this open and thin place, perhaps find faith for the first time.

Just as there can be ascent or descent in places of worship, the imagery of going up and down, steps or ladders, climbing or descending also permeates the language of the mystics. There is paradox here; in descending deep into ourselves, we also climb to the Divine. In going deep, even into the darkness of our fears, we find that God is there too; something captured in the poem *Beloved*:

...The way up is the way Down.
The ladder between heaven
and earth is everywhere present.
Go down to climb.
Descend to the last rung.
Descend into darkness, the bottom of
the pit and look,
what do you see?
Listen, what do you hear?
A light, a darkness that dazzles.
A voice, it has a voice.
A light in the darkness shining,
a light that is not light,
luminous of itself.
A voice, without sound, yet audible.
Where are You? Where are You?
"I am here, I am here, I am here!"

Jan van Ruysbroeck echoes this theme of ascending and descending, and the culmination of these climbs and falls is to discover our essential oneness in the Divine:

"...and so we are all a unity, being made one with Him in love...one love and one fruition: which fruition is consummated in the divine essence without mode of being. There we are all a simple and essential beatitude with God, without distinction, beatitude infinite and simple. There we are lost, drowned and liquefied into an unknown darkness."
[Jan van Ruysbroeck c1293-1381]

"Lost, drowned and liquefied into an unknown darkness" may sound terrifying to the uninitiated, but it is the contemplative Way that leads us here safely and into its beauty. Dwelling in this temple, the *con templum* of the divine presence, we think and act and feel in the world from a completely different place of being or plane of consciousness. It is the realm, the "Kingdom" (or "Queendom" in some views – see this subject explored in *Coming Home*) of heaven, the presence of the eternal now, the abiding love in which the community and connection of all is truly experienced. We come to live in a place in ourselves where there is no "now I am contemplating" and "now I am not contemplating". We break free of duality; the whole of life becomes contemplation, a condition of prayer "without ceasing".

Beginning and Ending in Prayer

...it follows that the whole salvation of man depends upon prayer and, therefore, it is primary and necessary, for by it faith is quickened and through it all good works are performed. In a word, with prayer everything goes forward successfully; without it, no act of Christian piety can be done. Thus the condition that should be offered unceasingly and always belongs exclusively to prayer."
[Anon. 19thC (The Way of the Pilgrim)]

Salvation, being "saved", is often difficult language to use in the modern era, but perhaps from the previous discussion and the more detailed exploration in Coming Home, it is clear what this is, the basis of the approach of the contemplative Way – it is that quality of being "drowned" in love, a love that loves to love, that is infinite and unknowable, present in us and intimately known. The transforming fire creates a knowing that we are loved by God completely as we are, that in our essence we are love and the unity of that love, ourselves and God in one. Love is the power that burnishes the ego of its worldly power, that severs the attachments that pull us away from the soul's longing for home. We are saved by love. Love calls unto love:

...the choiceless choice completes its inevitable story. Home. Home under the bell tower. Home in the bell. Union, communion, consummation. The ringing summons the next generation. And the next, down the long perplexing chain of ancestry. Love calls unto love. Left-behind unanswered questions reverberate in the recycle bin; cast away concerns of no relevance when the penny drops and realisation clunks against enlightenment. Questions and answers collapse into irrelevance, theology folds itself into redundancy. "What is God?" becomes an inflationary bagatelle when "Who asks the question?" is all the angels and saints can reply behind their upraised, gilded wings. Who calls to whom? Who speaks to whom? The divorce of personhood and time thus completed, the journey home resolved, who is left? Where do You end and we begin? We mirror You back to You. You, the seer and the seen. The glass mists, the image is lost, and left behind is only longing in boundless emptiness. Stars collide. A universe implodes, another bursts into time. And time drips away reducing everything to the same base metal. Everything seen in the same mirror, time's mirror, the cracked mirror splattered with shaving foam. Self and delusion of self collide like these stars, like these stains on the mirror. Only You. I knowing I. You knowing You. The cross legged contemplative sinks under the weight of magnificent possibility. Awestruck by truth, all matter having mattered, only stillness and listening remain. Stillness of body, stillness of mind. The space between the breath filled with everything, the stillness between the heartbeat replete with all possible motion. Duality empties. The darkness is illumined by complete darkness. Incomprehensible immobility grounds the temporary illusion of movement. You are what You always were, what You are, what You will be in that placeless place wherein "were" and "are" and "will be" have no grip. Only You. Such power to call Yourself. Power of faith, power of love. Love, invisible love, only You, only Love.

The above extract from the poem *Beloved* expresses something of that collapse of duality, the dissolution of separation from the Divine and the realisation of the power of love as the alchemical force that drives it. Lover and Beloved merge in the union of love:

"The pure, divine and liberated soul...will be gazed upon eternally in the same manner in which God is contemplated, and so enraptured will it be in this union that it will see itself as God, for God and the soul are one."
[JohannesTauler c1300-1361]

This growing sense of being saved by love, sometimes developing slowly, sometimes feeling like a lightning bolt of sudden deep realisation, is the contemplative Way. It is the rock on which the contemplative finds safe ground when buffeted by the storms of life and the interior struggle of going deeper into healing and love. There are times of bliss, but times of a fierce inner desert too. In *Coming Home* I explored how we may experience the desert in our lives, not just the waterless lands of the earth, but also the deserts of the soul, those times and places where we can feel abandoned, lost, hopeless – perhaps because of great fear and suffering. It can include feeling that God is unattainable or has rejected us or that we are not good enough. Or we are in pain and confused, feeling that we are not "doing it right" or unable to concentrate or lacking motivation. These are all common phenomena, the inner "demons", the dark nights of the soul and the senses that we must face, but which are also paradoxically rich material for us to take to God, our Soul Friend and Soul Community. The arid moments in our lives are not without hope. For it is here, in the dryness of the inner desert when it seems all else has failed, that there can be an inbreaking of divine love simply because all our defences are down.

Jesus exemplified this in his final prayer on the cross, "Father into your hands I commend my spirit" [Luke 23:46] – a profound prayer of complete acceptance, readiness to surrender into God, into the mystical marriage, when superficially all seems lost and suffering is at its greatest. The contemplative Way quietens the mind not to empty it but to drop it down into the heart, into the realm of feeling where God is known and experienced not as an abstract concept but as a true faith, a deeper level of knowing in relationship where lover and Beloved are one.

Like any marriage or intimate relationship we have to be prepared to work at it and find ways to sustain the bonding. For the contemplative, the bonds of the relationship are love and prayer:

> ***"In prayer the soul is cleansed from sin, pastured with charity, confirmed in faith, strengthened in hope, gladdened in spirit. By prayer the inward man is directed aright, the heart is purified, the truth discovered, temptation overcome, sadness avoided, the perceptions renewed, languishing virtue restored, lukewarmness dismissed, the rust of vices done away; and in it there do not cease to come forth living sparkles of heavenly desires, with which the flame of divine love burns. Great are the excellencies of prayer, great are its privileges! Before it Heaven is opened, secret things are made manifest, and to it the ears of God are ever attentive."***
> ***[St. Lawrence Justinian 1381-1456]***

Prayer is the medium of relationship to God, the thing that gets "sin" out of the way. I use sin here not in the limited, simplistic interpretation of doing or being "bad", but in the truest sense of the origins of the word. Early Greek translations of the bible use the word *hamartia* which means to "miss the mark", "be distracted", "miss the point". The English word sin comes from Old English *synn*. It is found in several other Germanic languages and comes from Indo-European roots concerned with qualities of "being" and "not being". Thus sinning in this sense, which lies at the root of the contemplative Way, is not so much concerned with moral lapses, but more about the nature of our consciousness. To sin is to miss the point, be distracted by trivia or ego seductions, not see or wander away from the truth of reality, of the Presence, of God's love.

Prayers of the heart have the power to break through the walls of "sin". One such prayer is drawn from the story of blind Bartimaeus in Luke [18:35-43] when he cries out to Jesus to have mercy (compassion) on him. It was developed further (and became known as the *Jesus Prayer*) through the seventh century writings of John Climacus and later embraced as a major spiritual practice in the church. It has variations on a theme but the words usually used are: "Lord Jesus Christ, Son of God, have mercy on me, a sinner." As western

Christianity pursued a more scholastic line after the schism with the Eastern Orthodox Church, it was in the latter that the practice of contemplation, using especially the Jesus Prayer, was retained and developed, reaching its apogee in the work of the monks of Mount Athos and its embrace in the Russian Orthodox Church. The latter is exemplified in the classic text the *Philokalia* (Greek:"love of the beautiful") a collection of works written between the fourth and fifteenth centuries by spiritual masters of the Christian contemplative, ascetic and *hesychast* (Greek: stillness, rest, quiet, silence) tradition.

The Jesus Prayer has seen something of a revival in recent years in Western Christianity. The archaic language can seem a little off-putting to some at first. For example, our understanding of "mercy" has tended to be distorted by views of mediaeval knights holding back from killing an opponent, but in fact the word means compassion, forgiveness or kindness. Compassion is more than feeling sorry for someone or having empathy for his or her plight. It is a willingness to act with love to help another. The blind beggar asks for Jesus' help quite directly. Thus on our spiritual search we learn to ask for help, to turn towards the Source, to acknowledge that we cannot do it all under our own steam, that we need the love of the Divine to save us from our doubts, distractions and disconnections.

In the book and CD *Song and Dance for the Way Home* I set some of these prayers in the form of chants with accompanying circle dances. Contemplation is also possible while moving physically and at the same time being inwardly still. The classic whirling dance of the Sufi is one such example of seeking union with the Divine through movement.

Many people are introduced to God as a separate, forbidding, remote power always ready to punish us. But a primary Christian message, indeed the message of many faiths, is that God is love. Furthermore, this love is not just general to all of creation but also specific to each one of us individually and uniquely. In the Old Testament Book of Isaiah [43:1-7] God speaks to the people Israel to remind them that they are called by name, that they are "precious to Me", they are loved and need not be afraid. I have often used this text to explore its rich symbolism with students (taken at face value, some of the language can again be difficult) not least to insert their own name in place of Israel. It can be life changing for some people to realise that they are personally, uniquely and individually loved by God. God says, "I love you", in this passage and these most powerful sacred words have become for me the simplest and most intimate of contemplations.

When all is said and done I am left with this personal prayer that transcends all others. What greater prayer can there be than "I love you"? Indeed if contemplation can be defined as anything it is about falling into the love of God, falling in love with God where each says to the other "I love you". Then there is nothing left but one "I love you". We fall into the love that loves us.

We have come full circle or perhaps completed a path around a spiral, coming to know our relationship with the Divine and yet not quite returning to the same place. God is infinite and the soul being of God is infinite too. There are no limits to our exploration of our relationship with, in and to God. But above and beyond all is a deep knowing of the love of God for us personally; coming to rest in this knowing we can let go of obstructions in ourselves. Healed by the love of God, we can love the Beloved completely as the Beloved loves us; and more, to love our neighbour as ourselves. It is the fulfilment of the contemplative prophecy.

It is a prophecy not about praying but about letting our whole lives become a prayer. This is *hesychasm*, the way of uncluttered stillness and repose that we seek in deep contemplation and into which prayer draws us. And the silence in God is profound, compared to it any silence in ourselves and the world is a cacophony. One who follows this path is a *hesychast* and he or she does so by prayer that cultivates *kenosis*, the emptying of the self in order to be filled with the Self. Some texts on this subject use the expression *anchoretism* (also having Greek origins, meaning withdrawal or retreat). Medieval England birthed one of the most famous anchorites who has influenced Christian spirituality across the world, Mother Julian of Norwich.

In withdrawing hermit-like either temporarily or permanently from worldly attachments and surrendering our identity to God we do not lose our freedom to be ourselves, we find it. It is the *fana' fi-l llah* of the Sufi's, the annihilation of all the distortions of identity and ego desires, everything into the beauty of the Divine beyond limited concepts of existence. On the Way Home the somebody that we have been with all its labels, man or woman, shopkeeper or surgeon, Christian or Hindu - the entire legion faces of the person, all are surrendered. Wealthy in identity, we do not get through the eye of the needle. Purified and surrendered of identity, we re-find our true identity, free of substance like the One from which we came; the tiniest door of time is now open to us:

> ***"It is in the depths of contemplation that love is discovered. Not the idea of love, beliefs about love or fantasy love, but love itself. Love has always been present, but unseen. It is not of this world, but can erupt into this world through us. Love is not an action, but action can be the fruit of love. Love, real love, is beyond words and concepts. It can only be tasted. It can be found at the heart of now, but only when one gives profound attention to what is."***
> ***[Simon Small 2007]***

The contemplative Way, as we deepen into it through discipline/discipleship, brings us to the place of integration. The contemplative is not someone who is praying all the time but someone who *is* prayer all the time, someone who has returned to him or herself. There evolves a way of being in the world where there is no "at the moment I am contemplating" and "at the moment I am shopping". As we go deeper into contemplative non-dual consciousness we find that the moments of forgetting tend to become less. Our lives shift from times of praying and not praying to an ever-deepening realisation that our life itself is a prayer. The contemplative Way becomes a condition of being, experienced in many ways. It is a way of consciousness that is not "here" or "there" or "then" and "now", but living each moment fully in God in which all time is held. Contemplation is to give sole (soul!) attention to that aspect of consciousness through which the "other" is experienced, fully, to be in a place where there is neither awareness plus activity nor awareness in activity but fully awakened consciousness in God. No here or there, but only the eternal now. Contemplation is the art of experiencing the ultimate reality of God in the depths of the present moment. For the contemplative, there is no this or that, there just is.

I can liken this to falling in love when no matter where we are or what we do the person is never "off our minds". As the love deepens and grows we know there are many times when we might forget the beloved person because we are required to think about/do other things, yet the love is so integrated that the beloved is with us even though our attention is elsewhere. A momentary pause, a switch of thinking and the beloved is re-membered once more; separation was just a thought away. The person we love does not reside solely in our thoughts but in our hearts, at a deeper level of consciousness than thinking. Thoughts come and go but the heart beats whether we pay attention to it or not and so does love of another person. How much more so is this when we are in the love of the Beloved?

The contemplative may have had to do much inner work of healing those wounds and misperceptions that are barriers to God. In other words, as I explained in *Coming Home*, it is not possible to bypass the emotional work. For example, if we have had punishing or shaming childhood experiences with authority figures such as parents, these lessons can be deeply ingrained. If unhealed, there is a tendency in later life to project these experiences onto the ultimate authority figure of God. Without liberation from these old wounds we can, for example, be led to assume that God may be loving, but is also a judging and punishing type who will do little more than belittle us and find fault or harm us in some way. Along with the emotional work, getting to know the God that is true evaporates the false God:

> ***...The first step is that of purest prayer. From this there comes warmth of heart, and then a strange, a holy energy, then tears wrung from the heart, God given. Then peace from thoughts of every kind. From this arises purging of the intellect, and next the vision of heavenly mysteries. Unheard of light is born from this ineffable, and thence, beyond all telling, the heart's illumination. Last comes – a step that has no limit though compassed in a single line – perfection that is endless..."***
> ***[Theophanis the Monk 1782-1884]***

Thus the practice of contemplation – paying attention, concentration, prayer, getting out of the way and surrender - is predicated upon an ever-deepening, on-going, healing and trusting relationship with the Divine. The work and effort prepares us for that relationship in which all our attention and awareness falls towards God, in which we come to know God more deeply. In doing so, paradoxically, we also come to realise, in humility, just how little we can know God. Yet the knowing is not facts or what the reason or the intellect can work out or deduce about God. No, the knowing is at an altogether different level, a knowing of profound love that transcends explanation. It transforms our way of being in the world. In the infinity of God, we experience an eternally evolving revelation where we come to grasp the true essence, the true being of things, ourselves and All-that-is.

The dialogue of Jesus with Pilate [John 18:37] comes to an impasse when different perceptions of truth arise, when the clash between reasoning our way and feeling our way to truth become incomprehensible to each other. The love of the contemplative is beyond intellectual reason and comprehension. It is a knowing of the heart, our very deepest self. We can seek to describe it (poets, artists, musicians often get closest) but it is essentially ineffable. Knowing that love and trying to pin it down is ultimately as futile as trying to prove that we love someone. We know when we love and we can describe some aspects of what it feels like or how it affects our behaviour towards the other, but ultimately describing love is impossible. Love is not to be defined, it is to be experienced.

Contemplation is falling in love with God, in which God works wonders on and with the soul. Just as we dedicate times of attention to a person when falling in love so that relationship can come to fruition and continue to evolve, so we must do the same in our relationship with God. Contemplation is that sacred attention, bringing our very heart and soul to God to discover the heart and soul of God. There is no end to getting to know God, to loving, to the relationship – rather it is one of endless expansion and unfolding, in love.

When we are in an intimate and loving relationship we know that no matter how long we have been together or how much we learn of each other, we are always learning something new. Love is the place of rest in relationship, it is also the place of movement, of growing into the place of love in the person (and in ourselves) not yet known to us; so it is with God. The contemplative Way is rooted in that wisdom. Having opened that Way in ourselves, it is God who transforms us. As we mature and heal in the love of God, we let go of the fear of love, fear of the limitless and boundless, and experience the joy of being limitless and boundless.

And what about those moments of forgetting, despair, distraction? These happen too in relationships. The contemplative Way embraces these moments as part of living a life permanently in God, sometimes seeming close, sometimes seeming remote. The endless push and pull, nearness and farness, are the very dynamics of the relationship, drawing us into ever-deeper discovery where we realise our birthright. Those spaces of forgetting or distraction are not occasions for blaming, judging or self-punishment but opportunities for joy; not "Oh, I've fallen away again, stupid me", but "Oh, there is a space where I forgot and I now have an opportunity to find God more." In this endless, passionate full-filling relationship we fall into the all-embracing "prison" that is love, the prison that is complete freedom:

> ***"If with God's help and without presumptuous reliance on his own efforts someone comes to win this condition, he will pass over to the status of adopted son. He will leave behind servility with its fear. He will leave aside the mercenary hope of reward, a hope which seeks a reward and not the goodness of the giver. There will be no more fear, no more desiring. Instead there will be the love which never fails."***
> ***[John Cassian c365-435]***

This is a fruit of the spirit, of becoming re-integrated with the source from which we came. We are made wealthy, wealthy beyond measure in love, the fire of love that has forged the reunion. Fear and desiring lose their grip on us. We inhabit and are inhabited by the love that never fails.

Part 2
Sacred Words – Suggestions for Contemplation

The words, such as those in the Jesus Prayer, are never treated as a set of syllables to quieten the mind. On that basis it would be a form of meditation where any sounds could be used. In some schools of meditation the words do not matter, what matters is the repetition of them. This is not the contemplative Way. The words and their meanings are crucially important, for they have their own power to transform consciousness. That is why the contemplative treats prayer words with enormous respect, for they are sacred words, not to be used flippantly.

Words that were once used only rarely, in special places such as monasteries and by initiates, are now commonplace. Spirituality in a world of mass and instant communication has broken down these limitations and is available to all. Yet that availability needs to be embraced with caution and respect, part of which is humility and the willingness to be subject to the guidance of others. The intellect cannot be inactive, so some of the words we use in our prayers give it something to do. Thus occupied and quietened, it is possible to plunge into a deeper level of consciousness. Yet the words do not leave us, they come with us into that depth, anchoring us, connecting us, inspiring us. The words are sacred for they signal our intention to turn towards God, to seek our centre.

Some of the earliest sacred words documented for the contemplative life are those used by John Cassian: "O God, make speed to save me: O Lord, make haste to help me" [Psalm 69:2]; sometimes simply rendered as "Come to my help, Oh God". In the writings of John Climacus and the *Philokalia* we encounter the Jesus Prayer. For many people the spiritual quest, the search for the Way Home, begins (or is given a push!) in moments that are challenging, when our old ways of doing things seem to come unstuck, when our customary values and perceptions are thrown into disarray. It can be extreme, feeling like we are drowning, under attack, overwhelmed and unable to cope as the storms of life batter us. We may feel disconnected from the Divine, abandoned, helpless, like we are "going under", alone – this can be a terrifying place to be: hell. These feelings may not just be a catalyst for the quest for they recur regularly along the Way.

In the New Testament [Matthew 14:30] one of the shortest of all prayers for just such a moment is made clear. To the astonishment of the disciples, Jesus walks across the sea to them amidst a storm. The disciple Peter attempts to walk on the water too, but he becomes distracted and frightened (off centre). His attention gone from Jesus, he soon sinks and is about to drown. He gasps, "Lord, save me!" Jesus reaches down and takes his hand.

The imagery is rich with symbolism. In stepping out of safe and known territory (the boat), we need help. The story exemplifies our limitations, our need to surrender and ask for help, in humility, to be open to the faith that there is One available to us willing to help. As we set out on the Way Home, we long to be free of suffering and the relentless drowning demands and desires of the ego, of everyday personhood and identity:

"An excessive multitude of words in prayer disperses the mind in dreams, while one short word or phrase helps to silence the mind"
[John Climacus c525-606]

In some traditions it is considered best to choose or be initiated into only one simple prayer and stick with it. Others encourage being open to words and phrases according to inspiration, perhaps after reading scripture in *lectio divina*. Other options include using a particular word and repeating it, such as *abba* (invoking the holy parent), *maranatha* or words such as God, Jesus, peace, love. Other traditions take this further and use the names or attributes of God and Jesus, perhaps words spoken by them or used about them. Such words are all used prayerfully, they are prayers of the heart, intended to help us go deep within. They steady us and focus our regard on God through the eye of the heart. By using prayers to God, even the names of God, we seek to be one with God. Contemplation, using sacred words, takes us into the heart of the heart. Sometimes we may use our breath to encourage this attention and allow the words to flow with its rhythm, perhaps while resting a hand upon the heart.

Prayers of the Heart

In the following pages I offer a few of the sacred words that I have personally found helpful, some handed down to me by my own teachers. It may be that you will find words here that are familiar to you and maybe you will feel an affinity for one or more that will become regular companions. Perhaps you will find it helpful to open one of these prayer pages and choose a prayer at random and make it your sacred words for that hour of prayer, or that day or that month.

Many of the sacred words below are arranged to align with the rhythms of the breath while sitting, but can also be matched to walking or other exercise and movement. Pray with what works. Sacred words are our invitation into relationship with God. In the end the form or the type of prayer becomes almost irrelevant as "deep calls unto deep" [Psalm 42] and we are drawn ever more into that Love we seek.

We can begin a prayer time with chosen words or they may hang on our lips every waking moment, but eventually they are put down as words in themselves. Perhaps you may need to ready yourself for prayer by using the preparation exercise described earlier. Experienced contemplatives may need no preparation time, but even the experienced can have occasions when they become ungrounded and need a simple exercise to call them Home.

Almost every one of the sacred words used here is taken directly or modified from the Old and New Testaments.

Prayers of preparation and connection: these can be used at any time of day or night to re-mind us of our relationship to God, to prepare us for the day or for a time of stillness and reflection, or before moving into a contemplative exercise:-

Beloved,
Break through the barriers that I erect between me and You.
Suffuse me with Your love, let nothing stand in the way.
Remove from my mind all distractions and inattention.
Open my eyes to see You,
My ears to hear You,
My mind to wonder at You,
My heart to know You,
Draw me along the Way into You.
Amen.

Beloved,
Help me to remember You
Until I forget to forget.
Amen.

Beloved,
May everything I say,
Think,
Feel and
Do,
Be Yours.
Amen.

Beloved,
Shine upon me, light of God.
Hold my heart, love of God.
Fire my soul, flame of God.
Wash away forgetting, water of God.
Blow away all fear, breath of God.
Ground me in your being, earth of God.
Unite me with you, grace of God.
Amen.

Beloved,
Help me turn to love when I want to turn away.
Help me take right action when I want to be selfish.
Help me be still when I want to run.
Help me to awaken when I want to sleep.
Amen.

Beloved,
When I cannot see the Way to go
Help me to trust in You.
When I cannot understand,
Help me to go on believing.
When all seems dark,
Let the light of faith shine in my heart.
Amen.

Beloved,
Walk with me and let me know Your peace.
Help my whole life be a prayer in You.
Draw my whole being to wait on You.
Help me to know Your will,
That I may serve.
Amen.

Beloved,
I see the waste land all about me.
Help me to see also the glory of creation, and the good in all beings.
Use me to play a part in the healing of the brokenness of Your world.
Help me to know that part and to be clear in Your will.
Strengthen me to follow Your will.
Amen.

Beloved,
Help me become who You want me to be.
Help me to help my neighbours become who You want them to be.
Help us transform Your world, and make it in the likeness of your heaven.
As above, so below.
Amen.

Beloved,
When I am in adversity, remind me of Your power.
When I am wandering, remind me of Your forgiveness.
When I am lonely, remind me of Your fellowship.
When I am sorrowful, remind me of Your comfort.

When I am above myself, help me to see You above me.
When I am beneath myself, help me to see You below me.
When I am beside myself, help me to see You at my centre.
When I am inside myself, help me to see You beyond me.

When I am feeling unloved, remind me of Your presence.
When I am feeling lost, remind me of Your way.
When I am feeling knowing, remind me of Your mystery.
When I am feeling hopeless, remind me of Your gift.
Amen.

Beloved,
Dissolve me in You
Break the chains that keep me trapped in my self.
Help me lose who I think I am,
And discover who I truly am,
In You.
Amen.

Beloved,
In the holy book help me to read You.
In the book of my life let me live You.
In the book of creation let me see You.
In the book of my neighbour let me love You.
Amen.

Beloved,
In my mornings let me awaken in You.
In my days let me awaken in You.
In my nights let me awaken in You.
In You let me find the eternal awakening.
Amen.

Beloved,
May I know Your peace that passes all understanding.
May I know Your transforming love.
May I know my image in You.
May I know all that I am in You.
Amen.

Beloved,
Nameless and unknowable,
Yet I call You by name,
And I long to know You.
Reach out and touch me,
Help me draw aside the veil of myself,
And fall into You.
Amen.

The following are simple prayers of the heart: to repeat, as often as wished, as an opening to contemplation. They lend themselves to repetition at any time of day or night, calling us Home when we have fallen into forgetting. These are just a few suggestions; scripture is full of possibilities that we can adapt ourselves. Some find it helpful to vary their prayer from time to time while others choose one prayer and stay with it (this is the tradition, for example, with the Jesus Prayer):-

"O God, make speed to save me: O Lord, make haste to help me"

"Breathe on me - breath of God."

"Lord Jesus, Christ, Son of God, have mercy on me, a sinner."

"Not my will - but Thine."

"Here I am, Lord"

"Come to my help, Oh God."

"Come, Lord Jesus."

"Lord, save me."

"Lord, help me."

Prayer names: although the following words are single names, each can be used as a prayer word. When speaking them, perhaps silently within ourselves, we can do so with a consciousness of desire to open to God, asking the Beloved to overcome our barriers, be present with us and our awareness of that presence to be deepened. So often God is seen as a remote being with whom we cannot have a personal relationship, yet time after time God directly or through the Christ addresses us individually. It's difficult to form a personal relationship when we use expressions such as Ultimate Reality or the Absolute, while names such as Beloved, Father or Mother suggest an intimacy – the God who is transcendent and immanent simultaneously. Although single words, they are asking words, relating words. Just as we may refer to a person by different names, so it is with God and each opens up possibilities of relationship. All can be aligned with the breath if you wish, for example by praying the single syllable words one with the in-breath and once with the out. The double syllable words can be prayed with the first syllable on the in-breath and the second with the out.

God

Presence

Jesus

Friend

Abba

Beloved

Lord

Mother

Father

Mary

Breath, Body and Sacred Words.

These words can be used as meditative exercises. Allow yourself to sit in silence and stillness with them. As you do so, place a hand over your heart, imagine yourself breathing these words into your heart. Use your breath to help the words flow ever deeper within. Each group of words permits the first part of the phrase to be spoken quietly within while breathing in: the second part is also spoken silently with the out-breath. Savour them; let them roll around in your consciousness as you repeat them. What meanings arise in them? How do they affect your relationship with God? Then let them go and just sit in God. Consider that with each phrase God is speaking to you personally – how does this affect you?

Another approach with some of these words is to use them to explore non-duality and the possibility of God in all things and all things in God, a subject addressed in more detail in *Coming Home*. Contemplation is not about hanging out with God then coming back into the world. It is hanging out with God and being in the world immersed in eternity and ordinary reality *at the same time*. Contemplation is being in all; that is non-duality. The world is in God and God is in the world, therefore all. To explore this you might, for example, hold the words when you are in a pleasant place, with someone you love or an image of God that is familiar to you. Then try holding them while looking at or thinking about something you find unpleasant such as rubbish in the street, a picture of a disaster or someone you dislike. It is easy to see God in the first. Can you also do so in the second? With each of these phrases, assume that it is God speaking to you:

Be not afraid –
it is I.

You are my beloved,
With you I am pleased.

Be still –
know Me.

I am here,
You are not alone.

Be still –
and know that I am God.

Allow the following words to go out to God and for them to return to you. As you breathe in, consider the first part to be spoken by God to you, as you breathe out allow the second part to be spoken back to God. Notice your responses.

Please allow me to share a couple of my personal favourites here. First of all is the simple "I am", which in Hebrew is *Ehyeh* (from *Ehyeh Asher Ehyeh* – "I am who I am" or "I shall be who I shall be". [Exodus 3:14]). Just sitting with the simplicity of that phrase, particularly in its original language, can be deeply centring. This is the God, the Beloved, the I-Amness that is both still and moving, full yet endlessly becoming, in eternity yet in time – mirroring the potential of our own I-Amness. Notice here the parallels with the "I Am" statements of Jesus in the final pages. Secondly, the God of the Israelites was given the personal name of *Yahweh*, drawn from the initials (YHWH) of words seeking to name the Divine rather than the words themselves. As God's name was regarded as too holy to be spoken the word "Lord" was often used. *Ehyeh* is the "I Am"; *Yahweh* is traditionally translated as "the One who brings into existence" or "the One who is becoming."

However, after many years of exploration, I find myself left with the purity of "I Love You" or the simple repetition of the holy name "Jesus". Perhaps all prayers, all efforts, come down to this the simplest prayer of the heart. The words are merely the vehicle carry us toward loving connection to the Beloved. Nothing is being requested, there is simply an exchange of deep truth, lover and Beloved become one.

You are My heart's desire -
You are my heart's desire.

You are the one I love -
You are the One I love.

You are the light -
You are the light.

I am here -
I am here.

You are My life -
You are my life.

You are the one I serve -
You are the One I serve.

I am-
I am.

You are My delight –
You are my delight.

Receive Me -
Receive me.

Come be with Me –
Come be with me.

I am becoming –
I am becoming.

Ehyeh –
Ehyeh.

I long for you –
I long for You.

I wait for you –
I wait for You.

Beloved-
Beloved.

You are the highest -
You are the highest.

I love you -
I love You.

All that I am is yours -
All that I am is Yours.

I surrender in you –
I surrender in You.

Yahweh -
Yahweh.

You are perfect –
You are perfect.

We are of one breath,
you and I -
We are of one breath,
You and I.

All of these words and phrases are taken from the Old and New Testaments, some with minor modification. In some cases there are numerous references to just one of the names or qualities of God, but I have given only one citation here otherwise this book would be a very long list (furthermore there are also many references to what God is not)! The list is not exhaustive, although most have been identified. I have included those with which I have personally worked and found most challenging or fulfilling. It is also worth noting that differences would occur with other Bible translations; throughout I have used the New Revised Standard Version (Anglicised).

One thing that may be apparent from this exercise is that God has many qualities and is a very active God in the world! No name can encompass God, but the words can point the way taking us from the familiar to the unknown. Chose one phrase and allow yourself to sit with the words. The Bible is replete with food for meditation at many levels, not least the names and qualities of God. May you find many teachings and blessings in them.

In his many books, Neil Douglas-Klotz has done more than anyone I know to open new vistas on scripture by his high quality work exploring the Hebrew and Aramaic roots. Alongside the works of Marcus Borg, JohnPhilip Newell Elaine Pagels, Cynthia Bourgault, Karen Armstrong, Evelyn Underhill and Jack Spong and cutting edge theologians like them, new riches are discovered that liberate us from the restricted God we often create for ourselves, a subject covered in more detail in *Coming Home*. The Douglas-Klotz book recommended in the bibliography contains a short but very illuminating dictionary of English, Hebrew and Aramaic words. The Aramaic versions of Bible texts explode with new possibilities of profundity and expansiveness.

Many religious leaders and books tend to have very definite views of what God is. Yet God, as we have explored in this book, is essentially unknowable. I have several maxims that inform my seeking and one of them is "Don't limit God". Contemplatives know something of the infinity of God and how unwise it is to try to define the Divine.

Many of the names or attributes of God given in the Bible do not always make comfortable reading. It is easy to work with words of love, light and glory, but how do we relate to a God who is described (or self-describes) as angry or jealous? It is best to be wary of attributing human qualities to God, or only placing our simplistic interpretations upon scriptural descriptions. Human feelings are often projected onto God, but in so doing we may inhibit our drawing closer to God. For example, "Fear" of God can be taken as trembling in terror because we are afraid God is going to zap us with punishment any minute. Some people do indeed see God like this, but that is not the God I know or experience. Fearful people will often see only a fearful God. If we expand our interpretation of fear (see *Coming Home*) as referring more to awe, reverence and humility before the Sacred, rather than being terrified, a whole new possibility of relationship opens to us.

For another example, consider the "jealous" God [Ex.34:14]. Does this refer to a temperamental being who will not tolerate any competition? Or does it say something about the fiery (loving) nature of God who helps us clear out from our consciousness all the false gods, distractions, attachments and distortions. The God of my life is jealous enough to have been the subversive who has undermined false gods such as the ill-tempered, bearded, old man up in the sky that I grew up with or my own "worship" of things material or superficial. The jealous God is a helping God, dissolving anything in ourselves and the world that seeks to stand against or split the essential wholeness of the Divine and our relationship to the Beloved.

In this section a series of statements from the Old and New Testaments describe what others say of God or what God says of the divine nature – thus the nameless One offers us words not to limit God, but to provide food for contemplation and a deepening relationship. I have abridged some from what would otherwise be long sentences.

You might begin by sitting with a phrase and simply repeating it a few times then falling into silence, with or without aligning it with your breathing. Or you might take one of the attributes of God such as "Peace" or "Love" and do the same. These are all meditations, based on the earlier definitions in the first chapter. They can be "worked on", but can be put down after a while and we can allow ourselves to move into wordless presence.

It is possible to combine all of them with the flow of the breath, for example (breathe in) "God is" (breathe out) "patient."; just breathing in and out with the words being spoken silently within, perhaps with hand on heart. Allow them to guide and illuminate your relating to God, to open you to God's presence by making a connection, showing up and taking an interest. How do you respond? What new insights arise? What do you feel? Then be still and let God be God.

Please note these are not offered as subjects for theological enquiry. That can be found elsewhere. Here, the words are invitations to approach God in relationship. Just as we get to know people from what they tell us about themselves and how we experience them, so it is with God. You might choose to work through these systematically writing your responses in your journal, sharing them with your Soul Friend and Soul Community. You might examine scripture to find other similar words and compare them or go to the original source and read around it. They can be explored at random, just by opening the page and placing your finger on it to choose your words for the day.

"I am" statements attributed to God:

I am the Alpha and the Omega. (Rev 1:8) • I am the first and the last. (Isa 44:6)

• I am God. (Isa 43:13) •

I am God Almighty. (Ge 17:1) • I am He. (Isa 43:10) • I am the Living One. (2 Esd 2:14)

I am the Lord. (Isa 42:8)

I am the Lord your God. (Lev 18:4) •
I am the One who knows and bears witness. (Jer 29:23) •
I am your Redeemer. (Isa 49:26) •
I am your Saviour.(Isa 49:26) •
I am your Shield. (Ge 15:1) •
I am who I am. (Ex 3:14) •

In many other passages God says something about what God is feeling or doing, and others also say what they believe God is:

God is able. (Mt 3:9)
God is an anchor. (Heb 6:10)
God is against. (Jer 23:32)
God is angry. (Nu 22:22)
God anoints. (1 Sam 26:10)
God appeals. (2 Cor 5:20)
God appears. (1 Ki 9:2)
God is awesome. (Ps 47:2)
God is beauty. (Ps 27:4)
God is beyond. (Ps 147:5)
God blesses. (Ge 1:22)
God is blessed. (1 Tim 1:11)
God breaks down. (Jer 45:4)
God breathes. (Ge 2:7)
God is breath. (Ecc 12:7)
God brings. (Job 8:7)
God builds. (Ezek 28:26)
God calls. (Isa 43:1)
God carries. (Isa 46:4)
God casts out. (Lev 18:24)
God chooses. (Ro 9:18)
God comforts. (Isa 49:13)
God is coming soon. (Rev 22:20)
God commands. (Deut 26:16)
God is compassion. (Jas 5:11)
God is compassionate. (Ex 22:27)
God is concerned. (1 Cor 9:9)
God condemns. (Job 10:2)
God is counsellor. (Isa 9:6)
God counsels. (Ps 33:11)

God covenants. (Ezek 16:22)
God creates. (Gen 1:1)
God is creator. (Isa 40:28)
God crosses over. (Job 9:3)
God curses. (Gen 12:13)
God defends. (Jdt 5:21)
God delights. (Ps 5:4)
God delivers. (Ps 140:7)
God demands. (Ezek 34:10)
God is depth. (1 Co 2:10)
God destroys. (Ezek 25:7)
God devises. (Mic 2:3)
God disperses. (Ezek 12:15)
God displays. (Ezek 38:23)
God drives out. (Dt 18:12)
God dwells. (Jn 14:10)
God is enthroned. (Ps 9:7)
God is exalted. (Ps 97:9)
God exiles. (Ezek 39:28)
God exists. (Ps 119:89)
God is everlasting. (Ps 90:7)
God is faithful. (1 Cor 1:9)
God is father. (Eph 4:6)
God fills. (Ps 81:10)
God is fire. (Ex 24:17)
God is first and last. (Isa 44:6)
God forbids. (1 Sam 26:11)
God forgives. (Ps 86:5)
God is a fortress. (Ps 71:3)
God is for us. (Ps 56:9)
God frees. (Ps 146:7)
God fulfils. (Jer 39:16)
God is fullness. (Eph 3:19)
God is fury. (Ps 2:5)
God gathers. (Isa 43:5)

God is generous. (Ro 10:12)
God gives. (Ecc 5:19)
God is glory. (Ps 19:1)
God is God. (Dt 7:9)
God is good. (Lk 18:19)
God is grace. (1 Pe 5:10)
God is gracious. (Ps 116:5)
God is great. (Dt 10:17)
God guides. (Isa 58:11)
God hates. (Dt 16:22)
God is the head of Christ. (1Cor 11:3)
God heals. (Ex 15:26)
God hears. (Ps 69:33)
God is in the heavens. (Ps 115:3)
God helps. (Ps 54:4)
God is high. (Mk 5:7)
God is holy. (Lev 11:44)
God is home. (Ps 68:6)
God is hope. (Ps 62:5)
God is immortal. (Ro 1:23)
God is in the midst. (Joel 2:27)
God inspires. (2 Ti 3:16)
God is invisible. (Col 1:15)
God is jealous. (Ex 34:14)
God is joy. (Ne 8:10)
God judges. (Ps 7:11)
God is justice. (Job 37:23)
God keeps. (Isa 42:6)
God is king. (Ps 10:16)
God knows. (Ps 94:11)
God is a lamp in the darkness. (2 Sam 22:29)
God leads. (Ps 23:2)
God is light. (1 Jn 1:5)
God is life. (1 Jn 5:20)
God listens. (Ex 22:27)

God lives. (2 Sam 2:27)
God lives in us. (1 Jn 4:12)
God is living. (Deu 5:26)
God looks. (1 Sa 16:7)
God is Lord. (Ps 33:12)
God is love. (1 Jn 4:8)
God makes. (Gen 14:19)
God manifests. (Ezek 28:22)
God is merciful (Ps 116:5)
God is mercy. (1 Chron 21:13)
God is mighty. (Rev 18:8)
God is in the midst. (Joel 2:27)
God is near. (Lk 21:31)
God is one. (Ro 3:30)
God opens the grave. (Ezek 37:13)
God is patient. (Ecc 18:11)
God is peace. (1 Cor 14:33)
God is perfect. (Mt. 5:48)
God plants. (Ezek 28:26)
God is pleased. (Mt 3:17)
God plucks up. (Jer 45:)
God is power. (Ps 63:34)
God is poverty. (Mt 22:29)
God praises. (Isa 42:8)
God prepares. (Ezek 39:17)
God is presence. (Ex 25:30)
God promises. (Nu 23:19)
God provides. (Josh 1:13)
God punishes. (Ex 32:34)
God purges. (Ezek 20:28)
God raises up. (Zech 11:16)
God is a redeemer. (Ps 19:14)
God reconciles. (Col 1:20)
God is refuge. (Ps 46:1)
God reigns. (Ex 15:18)

God rejoices. (Isa 62:5)
God releases. (Isa 61:1)
God requires. (Mic 6:8)
God rescues. (Ps 37:40)
God restores. (Ps 23:3)
God returns. (Mal 3:7)
God rewards. (Lk 6:23)
God is right. (Dan 9:14)
God is righteous. (Ps 11:17)
God roars. (Hos 11:10)
God is rock. (1 Sam 2:2)
God sanctifies (Lev 20:8)
God saves. (2 Chron 32:15)
God is salvation. (Isa 12:2)
God scatters. (Ezek 30:26)
God sees. (Gen 1:4)
God sends. (Jn 3:17)
God shakes. (Hag 2:21)
God shares. (Nu 18:20)
God shatters. (Dt 33:27)
God is a shield. (Ps 7:10)
God shows. (Ro 1:19)
God gives signs. (Isa 7:14)
God is slow to anger. (Ex 34:6)
God is sorry. (Ge 6:7)
God is sovereign. (Rev 6:10)
God speaks. (Ex 20:1)
God is spirit. (Jn 4:24)
God stirs up. (Jer 51:1)
God is a stranger. (Mt 25:35)
God is strong. (Ps 140:7)
God strengthens. (Isa 41:10)
God strikes. (1 Sam 26:10)
God is a stronghold. (Ps 9:9)
God summons. (Jer 25:29)

God is sun and shield. (Ps 84:11)
God surrounds. (Ps 125:2)
God swears. (Ezek 20:42)
God takes away. (Ezek 24:16)
God takes by the hand. (Isa 42:6)
God teaches. (Ps 86:11)
God tests. (Job 13:3)
God threatens. (Ezek 6:10)
God is true. (Jn 3:33)
God is trust. (Ps 111:7)
God turns. (Dt 23:5)
God is understanding. (Job 36:5)
God upholds. (Isa 42:1)
God is vengeance. (Ps 94:1)
God vindicates. (Job 13:18)
God is the vinegrower. (Jn 15:1)
God waits. (Sus 1:59)
God is a warrior. (Ex 15:13)
God is the way. (Ps 86:11)
God watches. (Ps 1:6)
God is weary. (Jer 15:6)
God wills. (Mt 6:10)
God is winged. (Ps 17:8)
God is wise. (Ro 16:27)
God is witness. (Ge 31:50)
God is with us. (Mt 1:23)
God is wonderful. (Isa 9:6)
God is the Word. (Jn 1:1)
God works. (Ge 2:2)
God is in the world. (Jn 1:10)
God is worthy. (2 Sam 22:4)
God wounds. (Dt 32:39)
God is wrath. (La 4:11)
God is zeal. (Isa 37:2)

Jesus says of Himself:

I am from above. (Jn 8:23)
I am alive for ever and ever. (Rev 1:18)
I am the Alpha and the Omega, the first and the last, the beginning and the end. (Rev 22:13)

I am with you always. (Mt 28:20)
I am among you as one who serves. (Lk 22:27)
I am ascending to my Father and your Father,to my God and your God. (Jn 20:17)

I am baptised. (Mk 10:39)
I am the bread of life. (Jn 6:35)
I am coming soon. (Rev 22:12)
I am coming to you. (Jn 14.18)

I am doing. (Lk 20:8)
I am in my Father, and you in me, and I in you. (Jn 14.20)
The Father is in me and I am in the Father. (Jn 10.38)

For where two or three are gathered in my name, I am there among them. (Mt 18.20)
I am giving you these commands. (Jn 15.17)
I am going to the father. (Jn 15:10)
I am God's Son. (Jn 10:36)
I am going to him who sent me. (Jn 7:33)
I am deeply grieved; even to death. (Mt 26:38)
I am he. (Jn 4;26)

I am here. (Jn 8:42)
I am from Him. (Jn 7:29)
I am Jesus of Nazareth. (Acts 22.8)
I am the light of the world. (Jn 8:12)

I am the living bread. (Jn 6:51)
Before Abraham was I am. (Jn 8:58)
I am the gate for the sheep. (Jn 10:7)

I am the good shepherd. (Jn 10:11)
I and the Father are one. (Jn 10:30)
I am not alone because the Father is with me. (Jn 16.32)

I am the resurrection and the life. (Jn 11:25)
I am the root and the descendant of David, the bright morning star. (Rev 22:16)

I am sending you out. (Lk 10:3)
I am sending upon you what my father promised. (Lk 24:29)
I am standing at the door, knocking. (Rev 3:20)
I am thirsty. (Jn 19:28)
I am the way, the truth and the life. (Jn 14:6)
I am the true vine. (Jn 15:1)
I abide in you. (Jn 15:4)

Part 3

Endpiece

As I completed Contemplation in 2017, there was much media commentary suggesting we live in a time of unprecedented global turmoil, political upheaval and danger. The only news seemed to be bad news. Yet the reality is that human beings have never lived longer and in less warlike times than we do now, while the Anthropocene Age is simultaneously taking our world into the uncharted territory of climate change.

The response to numerous perceived threats has led to a shift in many countries towards authoritarian and 'populist' politics. Mishra's *Age of Anger* is upon us, driving *ressentiment*, a raging inclination to blame others for our ills rather than face up to our own failings and inner shadow. He sees the need for a re-enchantment of our worldview, a re-spiriting of relationships with each other and All-that-is, which will help us transform such crises. Hariri's *Homo Deus* also looks from past to future and offers a dialectic of humanity evolving as a collection of mechanistic algorithms; artificial intelligence may subsequently render us redundant, or rather become us.

Mishra and Hariri are part of a long chain of intellectuals down the years who have sought to explain the human condition and peer into our future. While solutions to our problems are specific to our time, there is a sense of an undercurrent, a continuity, a perennial philosophy that may shift in its pattern, but is at its root the same down all the ages. That is the contemplative way.

Perhaps it is no coincidence that we are witnessing a worldwide increase in interest in contemplation; a counterbalance to the unleashed shadows of despair and despotism. Perhaps because it offers the re-enchantment of humanity that Mishra posits.

Those who are engaged in Coming Home to themselves are the contemplatives of this world. They reject the dystopian embrace of the divided self, the pessimism and cynicism of a world without meaning or purpose and bereft of Presence or consciousness other than that of the little or false self. To the contemplative, consciousness is infinitely more wonderful than that offered by so much of psychology or neurology. The contemplative sees all things connected in this sacred wonder. There is no place that the Beloved is not, no site that is more sacred than any other. Wherever they stand they stand on holy ground, in themselves and the world.

Contemplation offers hope in this and all epochs, for it is not a flight from the ordinary reality, but a deeper engagement with it from a place of inner wholeness, unitive consciousness and compassionate action. Contemplatives tend not to want 'power over' others but open to 'power under', in service. They have no interest in the exploitation of the natural world, but seek its healing and wholeness, recognising the interconnectedness and sacredness of all things. They do not see violence as a means of change, do not go to war or seek to create the world in their image, feel no desire to exploit others. They do not become suicide bombers, sexual predators, power-hungry demagogues or destroyers of species. They have no interest in superficial ego desires, no desire to control others, no wish to be 'in charge'. Their longing is for connection; their desire is for justice, their work is towards community and collaboration.

All of this is grounded in the very Source of life itself in which they live and move and have their being and which lives and moves and has being in each one of us, all of us, if we would but wake up to that truth. The contemplative touches the very ground of being, rests in the Divine unity from which all flows and to which all returns. In this here and now there is no lack, but love abundant and available for all. Who would have 'needs' when fed by such a living, eternal stream?

The contemplative subverts prevailing ways of seeing themselves and the world. They tend not to be interested in borders between peoples or artificial and reductionist ego-constructs of identity. The contemplative says from a condition of non-dual consciousness, "I am, therefore I think. I am, therefore I love. I am therefore I serve."… and recognises these words echo throughout All-that-is. The contemplative is stillness in movement, simplicity amidst complexity, humility in the face of ego-inflation. The contemplative is not just interested in who we are, but also who we might be; not just interested in their own awakening, but in the awakening of all.

Contemplation is not escapism or retreat into an idealised past, but a perennial truth available in all times and in all places. Like an underground river, it is invariably hidden, yet subtly feeding the wells of life wherever it is needed. It is an answer, perhaps the answer, to the connecting of all peoples of all faiths and none, carrying its essential wholeness and integration to all that it touches. It is a way of healing the brokenness of the world and ourselves. Its time is always now.

Bibliography

All Bible references are taken from the New Revised Standard Version (Anglicised)

à Kempis T (trans. Croft A & Bolton H) 2004 The imitation of Christ. Hendrickson. Peabody
Abhishiktananda 1967 Prayer. ISPCK. Delhi
Alcantara, Peter of (trans. Hollings G) 1904 A golden treatise on mental prayer. Mowbray. London
Anon. (trans. Wolters C) 1978 The cloud of unknowing. Penguin. Harmondsworth
Anon. (trans. French R) 1991 The way of the pilgrim. Harpercollins. New York
Anthony, Abbot cited in Merton T 1960 The wisdom of the desert. New Directions. New York
Armstrong K 1993 A history of God. Heinemann. London
Ashwin A 1990 From pain into prayer. Fount. London
Athanasius (trans. Gregg R) 1980 The letter to Marcellinus. Paulist. New York
Becket, Sister Wendy 1994 The gaze of love. Harper. San Francisco
Benedicta Sister/Edith Stein (trans. Anon.) 1992 The hidden life: hagiographic essays, meditations, spiritual texts. Province of Discalced Carmelites. Washington (available at http://www.karmel.at/ics/edith/stein.html)
Bingen, Hildegard of (trans. Davies O) 2005 Selected writings. Penguin. London
Blois, Louis of (trans. Bowden J) 2009 Spiritual works of Louis of Blois, Abbot of Liesse. Kessinger. Whitefish
Boehme J (trans. Erb P) 1977 The way to Christ. Paulist. New York
Borg M 1997 The God we never knew. Harpercollins. San Francisco
Borg M 1989 The heart of Christianity. Harper. San Francisco
Bourgeault C 2008 The wisdom Jesus. Shambhala. Boston
Cassian J (trans. Luibheid C) 1985 Conferences. Paulist. New York
Clairvaux, Bernard of (trans. Evans G) 2005 Selected works. Harper. San Francisco
Climacus J (trans. Luibheid C & Russel N) 1982 The ladder of divine ascent. Paulist. New York
Dalrymple J 1984 Simple prayer. DLT. London
de Chardin T (trans. Wall B) 1960 The phenomenon of man. Collins. London
de Chardin T (trans. Vann G) 1970 Hymn of the universe. Fontana/Collins. London
de l'Incarnation, Marie (trans. Mahoney I) 1989 Selected writings. Paulist. New York
de Spinoza B (ed. Morgan M) 2002 Spinoza: complete works. Hackett. Cambridge
Dionysius the Areopagite (trans. Luibheid C) 1989 Paulist. New York
Dodson P & Tunnicliffe M 2005 Exploring contemplative prayer. Mayhew. Stowmarket
Dossey L 1996 Prayer is good medicine. Harper. San Francisco
Douglas-Klotz N 1999 The hidden gospel. Quest. Wheaton
Eckhart, Meister (trans. Davies O) 1994 Selected writings. Penguin. London
Eliot T 1944 The four quartets. Harcourt Brace Jovanovich. London
Foligno, Angela of (trans. Steegman M) 1909 The book of divine consolation. Kessinger. Whitefish
Garrigou-Lagrange R (trans. Cummins P) 1952 Life everlasting and the immensity of the soul. Tan. Rockford.
Garrigou-Lagrange R (trans. Doyle M) 2003 Christian perfection and contemplation. Tan. Rockford
Genoa, Catherine of (trans. Hughes S) 1986 Purgation and purgatory: the spiritual dialogue. SPCK. London
Guyon, Madame (trans Guyon J) 2001 Experiencing union with God through inner prayer. Bridge-Logos. Alachua
Hadewijch (trans. Hart C) 2006 The complete works. Paulist. New York
Hariri Y 2017 Homo Deus. Vintage. London
Hilton W (trans. Anon.) 2004 The ladder of perfection. Kessinger. Whitefish
Keating T 1994 Intimacy with God. Crossroad. New York
Lanzetta B 2015 Path of the heart. Blue Sapphire. San Diego
Lawrence, Brother (trans. Anon.) 2004 The practice of the presence of God. Hendrickson. Peabody
Lisieux, Therese of (trans. Taylor T) 2006 The story of a soul. Kessinger. Whitefish
Magdeburg, Mechtilde of (trans. Tobin F) 1998 The flowing light of the godhead. Paulist. New York
Main J 1998 The inner Christ. DLT. London
McEntee R & Bucko A 2015 The new monasticism. Orbis. New York
Merton T 1949 Seeds of contemplation. Hollis & Carter. London
Merton T 1960 The wisdom of the desert. New Directions. New York

Merton T 1973 Contemplative prayer. DLT. London
Mishra P 2017 Age of anger. Allen Lane. London
Newell J P (1997) Listening to the heartbeat of God. SPCK. London
Norwich, Julian of (trans. Doyle B) 1983 Meditations. Bear. Santa Fe
Origen (ed. McGuckin J) 2004 The Westminster handbook of Origen. Knox. London
Pagels E 2006 The gnostic gospels. Phoenix. London
Panikkar, Brother Raimon (trans. Cunneen J) 2006 The experience of God. Fortress. Minneapolis
Porete M (trans. Crawford C) 1990 A mirror for simple souls: the mystical work of Marguerite Porete. Crossroad. New York
Poulain A (trans. Anon.) 1910 The graces of interior prayer. Kessinger. Whitefish
Ramon, Brother 1999 The flame of sacred love. BRF. Oxford
Ramon, Brother & Barrington-Ward S 2001 Praying the Jesus Prayer together. BRF. Oxford
Robin M (trans. Blake M) 1980 Marthe Robin and the foyers of charity. Theotokos. London
Rolle R (trans. Misyn R) 2005 The fire of love and the mending of life or the rule of living. Kessinger. Whitefish
St. Augustine (trans. Warner R) 1963 The confessions. Penguin. New York
St. Bonaventure (trans. Cousins E) 1978 The soul's journey into God. Paulist. New York.
St. Catherine of Siena (ed. O'Driscoll M) 1993 Catherine of Siena: passion for the truth, compassion for humanity: selected spiritual writings. New City. New York
St. Clare of Assisi (trans. Armstrong R) 2006 The lady: Clare of Assisi - early documents. New City. New York
St. Francis of Assisi (trans. Robinson P) 2007 The writings of St. Francis of Assisi. Forgotten. Marston Gate.
St. Ignatius of Loyola (trans. Puhl S) 2000 The spiritual exercises of St. Ignatius. Vintage. New York
St. Isaiah the Solitary (in St. Nikodimos & St. Makarios (trans. Palmer G, Sherrard P & Ware K) 1979 The Philokalia. Faber & Faber. London
St. John of the Cross (trans. Zimmerman B) 1973 The dark night of the soul. Clarke. Cambridge
St. John of the Cross (trans. Carrigan H) 2002 The ascent of Mount Carmel. Paraclete. Brewster.
St. Lawrence Justinian (trans. Kirsch J) 1910. St. Lawrence Justinian in The Catholic Encyclopaedia. Appleton. New York
St. Mary Magdalene de Pazzi (ed. Socias J) 2003 Daily Roman Missal. Midwest Theological Forum. Chicago
St. Nikodimos and St. Makarios (trans. Palmer G, Sherrard P & Ware K) 1979 The Philokalia. Faber and Faber. London
St. Theresa of Avila (trans. van de Weyer R) 1995 The interior castle. Harpercollins. London
St. Theophan, the Recluse (trans.Williams E) 1990 The life and teachings of St.Theophan, the Recluse. PIP. South Brent
St. Thomas Aquinas (trans. Clark M) 2000 An Aquinas Reader: Selections from the writings of Thomas Aquinas. FUP. New York
Small S 2007 From the bottom of the pond. O Books. Winchester
Spong J 2007 Jesus for the non-religious. Harper. San Francisco
Spong J 2010. Newsletter via Everyday Health. North Adams. August 5th 2010
Tallis T (composed c1590) 2001 Spem in alium. The Tallis Scholars. Phillips. London
Tauler J (trans. Shrady M) 1985 Sermons. Paulist. New York
Taverner J 1988 The protecting veil. Chester Music. London
Temple R 1990 Icons – the mystical origins of Christianity. Element. Shaftesbury
Theophanis the Monk (trans. Palmer G, Sherrard P & Ware K) 1984 The ladder of divine graces. in St. Nikodimos and St. Makarios (trans. Palmer G, Sherrard P & Ware K) 1984 The Philokalia. Faber & Faber. London
Torkington D 1995 The mystic – from charismatic to mystical prayer. Hodder & Stoughton. London
Torkington D 1999 The hermit – a personal discovery of prayer. Alba House. New York
Torkington D 1999 The prophet – the inner meaning of prayer. Alba House. New York
Trinity, Elizabeth of the (trans. Kane A & Nash E) 1984 Complete works. ICS. Washington
Underhill E 2003 Mysticism. One World. Oxford
van Ruysbroeck J (trans. Sherwood-Taylor F) 1944 The seven steps of the ladder of spiritual love. Dacre. London
von Goethe J (trans. Stopp E) 1998 Johann Wolfgang von Goethe maxims and reflections. Penguin. London
Weil S (trans. Crawford E & von der Ruhr M) 2002, Gravity and Grace. Routledge & Kegan Paul. New York
Wright S G 2010a Burnout – a guide. SSP. Penrith
Wright S G 2010b Beloved. SSP. Penrith
Wright S G 2017 Coming Home – notes for the journey. SSP. Penrith
Wright S G 2005 Reflections on spirituality and health. Wiley. Chichester
Wright S G & Sayre-Adams J 2009 Sacred Space – right relationship and spirituality in health care. SSP. Penrith

I promised you: I keep my promises.
"My Word shall not return to Me void."
In the silent inner chamber of your heart
you will hear everything you need to hear.
How does that sound?
I'll answer that for you;
you'll hear something no one has ever told you about.
The sound of Love.

Stephen works as a spiritual director and teacher for the Sacred Space Foundation (www.sacredspace.org.uk), guiding group retreats and individual seekers. Before this he had a long and distinguished nursing career in practice and academia gathering an extensive list of publications, an MBE, a Fellowship of the Royal College of Nursing and lots of other letters before and after his name along the way. His life and path of service took a significant about turn with a series of profound and transformative spiritual experiences that led him into giving more time, among other things, to the integration of spirituality into health care – for which he was later made an Honorary Fellow of the University of Cumbria. He has written three books exploring the nature of healing relationships - *Therapeutic Touch* and *Sacred Space – right relationship and spirituality in health care* (both with Jean Sayre-Adams) and *Reflections on spirituality and health*. He continues to work in the UK's NHS in "Heartfullness" educational programmes for healthcare professionals (see youtu.be/YUMBKXjgEN0). Coming Home is rooted in a personal, and continuing, account of spiritual awakening and his work as a spiritual director. For the latter he has received significant training in the presence of several renowned teachers and at the Interfaith Seminary (now OneSpirit) in the UK. His other recent published works include a CD of chants and circle dances (*Song and dance for the Way Home*), poetry (B*eloved* and *Yours, Faithfully*), *Burnout* and *Coming Home*. He lives with his partner in the English Lake District, deepening service and spiritual practice, participating in his local church community and the Iona Community, taking care of his organic garden and enjoying grandfatherhood.

43900292R00080

Made in the USA
Middletown, DE
22 May 2017